Every Little Thing Matters

First published by O Books, 2010
O Books is an imprint of John Hunt Publishing Ltd., The Bothy, Deershot Lodge, Park Lane, Ropley,
Hants, SO24 0BE, UK
office1@o-books.net
www.o-books.net

Distribution in:

UK and Europe
Orca Book Services Ltd
tradeorders@orcabookservices.co.uk
directorders@orcabookservices.co.uk
Tel: 01235 465521 Fax: 01235 465555
Int. code (44)

USA and Canada
NBN
custserv@nbnbooks.com
Tel: 1 800 462 6420 Fax: 1 800 338 4550

Australia and New Zealand
Brumby Books
sales@brumbybooks.com.au
Tel: 61 3 9761 5535 Fax: 61 3 9761 7095

Far East (offices in Singapore, Thailand,
Hong Kong, Taiwan)
Pansing Distribution Pte Ltd
kemal@pansing.com
Tel: 65 6319 9939 Fax: 65 6462 5761

South Africa
Stephan Phillips (pty) Ltd
Email: orders@stephanphillips.com
Tel: 27 21 4489839 Telefax: 27 21 4479879

Text copyright Stephen Oakes 2009

Design: Tom Davies

ISBN: 978 1 84694 423 9

A CIP catalogue record for this book is available
from the British Library.

Printed by Digital Book Print

O Books operates a distinctive and ethical publishing philosophy in
all areas of its business, from its global network of authors to
production and worldwide distribution.

Every Little Thing Matters

Stephen Oakes

BOOKS

Winchester, UK
Washington, USA

CONTENTS

This book is dedicated to my teacher and friend Hazel Raven. I have benefitted so much from her kindness, generosity and warmth, as I have from her vast knowledge of and connection to Spirit.

What I call 'Energy Work' I learned from Hazel, and what a wonderful mentor she is, full of wit and honesty. I learned more energy truth from Hazel than in all my life previously.

Hazel always was and remains my inspiration, and I aspire to work as tirelessly and effectively as her in bringing the message of Spirit down to Earth.

I am both blessed and gifted to have Hazel as part of my life.

Thank you Hazel.

Namaste.

Introduction.

For all the sophistication of our modern world, there is precious little education in a most vital area, the interface between higher energy and the physical body, the 'Human Energy Field.'

It is widely known that the world needs more compassion, kindness and love. Most of us, at least those that care, aspire to gaining more of what we call 'Spirituality.' We read books about the power of 'Now', we learn that all we need to achieve more is more meditation. All we need to do is to 'allow' and the law of Intention and the Universe will supply the rest.

All well and good, and we believe these authors to be good and true, and it is plainly obvious that they have 'made it' by utilising these very laws. So we apply ourselves diligently to these tenets and push hard to do exactly what we are being told is necessary for the success that we so crave.

So why is it that the promised results only happen sporadically, or even not at all, or more strangely, not in the fashion or way that we thought we had intended? The same writers assert that we must be eternally patient whilst we are practising to succeed, and that the answer is that we practise the techniques more so, and with more concentration. So why do these methods appear not to work for us? We have tried our hardest and assiduously applied ourselves, haven't we?

Disappointment abounds as we conclude that it is our 'Karma' that is against us, that the powers that be are punishing us, or that we are 'not good enough.' We head back to the bookshop or the internet for another book, another sure-fire method that will catapult us into happiness and success. We search for another way to produce the results that we desire 'now.' How often though do we end up with a bagful of good intentions, a shelf or two full of books, and the same-old, same-old?

Why is this so often the truth? What do the people who have made it work have that we do not? Have they a secret power, a broadband connection to God?

I am here to tell you that there is no 'secret' power, nor any bar on you having your desires. What is happening is that the people who have made it have something that we do not have, *yet!* They have a fully-functioning and connected to source-energy Human Energy Field, or H.E.F. They have a powerful connexion to spirit, or source, and they are effective transmitters of that energy. They've got it going on!

This is the vital education that is missing from the many spiritual books that we have read. We have to have a fully-functioning and unblocked H.E.F. to connect to source and bring down into our lives the very energy that will transform our lives, and allow us to fully activate those amazing spiritual laws that the teachers have told us about.

So here is your practical, friendly, easy to understand guide to the Human Energy Field (H.E.F.), the vital interface between your Immortal Soul and your physical body, the only effective and repeatable pathway for the true power of 'source' energy to enter into our lives *now!*

This guide will stop you worrying that you aren't doing 'enough,' or 'the right thing,' to progress spiritually in your life. A guide that will educate and support you as you begin your journey into energy freedom and your true self, a guide that is your 'Energy Work 101.' So take a step back from the rigours of day-to-day life and gently say to yourself; *"I am here today; I have made it this far, thank you."*

You have made it, and whatever has befallen you on your journey to reading these words, you have survived in a difficult world. That is a miracle, as all of life is a miracle. Thank the process that got this book to you. Thank the people that taught and inspired you. Thank the people that got these words into this book and onto the bookshelves. Thank source for the sequence of events that got you reading these words, even if you are only browsing. For you were made for greatness, you came from greatness, and greatness is yours, it is your birthright.

BUT...... (There has to be one!)

You have to start somewhere!

Start by reading this book....

Chapter One

You and your Human Energy Field.

'Here' and *'Now.'*
On this small blue planet in the 21st Century we are living in a technologically advanced society that is burdened with surveillance and monitoring of our activities. We are visually and aurally dominated by a worldwide media that bombards us 24/7 with images of pain and suffering, death and degradation. This is called 'news' and we are supposed to watch and listen intently. War continues to rage in many places on the planet, and our politicians tell us that there is nothing they can do to end these wars except to send more troops, to end the war.

More than any other time in recorded history our society is awash with electrical gadgets and fancy goods, computer consoles and toys for our children; food and drink are cheap and readily available. We can fly relatively cheaply all over the world; we have the Internet and thus instant communication with anywhere else in the world. We can aspire to and gain vast wealth and great properties in large tracts of land. What more could we ask for?

Yet there is a collective sigh that is coming from the soul of humanity, a metaphoric hole in the heart of the human race. Something is missing from our lives. Many of us have a sense of this without knowing why, you can feel it in the air, see it on others faces. We all wonder why there can't be peace and understanding in the world, why can't governments sort out our differences and show us the way to peace. After all we are all just people aren't we?

The stress of this puts a strain on everything we do in the chaotic energy caused by the maelstrom of 'wrong things' projected at us everyday. We glare at the person ahead of us in the supermarket queue, 'Hurry up, I haven't got all day!' Traffic causes us angst as we rush to get home. Sitting in front of our digital TV's with telephones nearby and on extension lines in most rooms. Computer constantly connected to broadband lines with e-mail at the ready. Mobile phones sat close by to send those urgent texts that we need to do. Credit cards bursting at their limits but flexed and ready to pounce, eager to buy that 'must-have' on e-bay. Fridge-freezers chock full of food, beer, wine and other goodies, hypermarket five minutes away by car if we run out of anything.

What could possibly be missing? But there it is again, that nagging feeling of doubt or guilt, a sense that we have forgotten something, or neglected an area of our lives perhaps? And it won't go away; no matter how much we apply Yoga, Pilates, Kickboxing or Jogging, we cannot remove it. So we apply alcohol, nicotine, chocolate, sweets, more food and even drugs. We go to the doctor who gives us pharmaceuticals to fix the hole, to 'attack' our depression, and rid us of the 'headache' that simply being alive has caused. But still the void within remains and it is an untouchable emptiness that we struggle to define.

You would think that with all of the information at our fingertips it would be easy to find out the answer. After all, it usually only takes us a couple of clicks to learn about anything from the Internet search engines, doesn't it? But there isn't a readily available answer that will fix that void within. At least there hasn't been; not until now that is.

Where are you reading this book? Perhaps you are travelling on a plane or sitting in a train? Sipping a Latte in a café? Relaxing in a hot bath, or sitting in a chair with a cup of tea and biscuits at hand? Wherever you are on this beautiful planet that we share, however you feel, right now, you are the sum total of all your experiences, choices and memories. The only person in the world that knows how you truly feel right now is you. Only you know the insecurity and pain that your life has seemingly thrown into your path. Only you remember the knockbacks and the slights, the insults and the injuries, the disappointments that have tainted the joys.

I'm sure that you have shared your pain and joys with close friends, and that is a comfort. Family may have helped here too; they may also have been the problem. Maybe career, college or work hasn't worked out, or money could be the bugbear that is grinding at you. There are many factors that affect us and deplete our energy, and they all share two things; they are unique to us and they have taken time to develop in our lives.

You might be sitting on a park bench chewing on your pastrami and rye with one pound in your pocket next to a tramp with a million pounds in his offshore accounts, but you both share the same pain, the same feeling that 'something' is missing. Happiness and fulfilment always seem to be 'out-there,' in fact you are constantly told that everything is 'out-there' for you, that success and wealth are waiting 'out-there' for you, love is 'out-there,' opportunity and a satisfying career are 'out-there' ripe for the picking. But where is 'out-there'?

If you walk a mile from where you are now, will you then be at 'out-there'? If not, how far is it to 'out-there' and which direction should we choose? Why won't somebody tell us, shouldn't there be signposts? "Only two more working weeks and heartbreak till you get to 'out-there' don't let's give up now!" Well wherever this mythical place is, it never stops us from pushing harder against the lack of fulfilment, whilst praying and hoping that the 'it's all' that is 'out-there', we are reliably informed 'for-us' will 'find-us' and 'sooner rather than later'!

The trouble with this is that however much we think, plan, push and grind, the fickle hands of destiny and fate slap us back to where we started. The same disappointments come round again and again, the same person turns up at your door dressed in a different body with a different name but offering the same old relationships. You must be sick of it by now? I mean I'm sick of it for you, and I like the look of your sandwich too!

So, what to do? Are we locked solidly into a world of misery, a hamster-wheel of joyless doing and working, servicing our credit debts and mortgages, 'making-do' and compromising, accepting the inevitable daily grind into an almost welcome senility? Stuart Wilde calls this the world of 'tick-tock' living, others call it the 'circle-world' I've called it...well I'd better not say, this is a family show after all.

The very reason that 'tick-tock' works so well and has so many unwilling subscribers is that the task of turning it all around seems so enormous. It takes a brave human-being to look in the mirror and name all their faults. In truth most of us hide in our disappointments, running them again and again on the movie screens of our memory banks, weeping at the same places and wringing of hands at the appropriate points. We nominate a 'big-fix' that will sort it all out, a magical swipe of destiny's wand that will cure all of our woes. It could be the 'perfect' lover, the 'dream' job, the 'life-changing' windfall, the 'happy' home. We cling and hope against hope that they will 'drop' into our lives, and when they don't we are back on the park bench silently weeping into our Pastramis.

There's a great line in Pink Floyd's song 'Time' that describes being locked in the circle world perfectly, it goes like this,

"Ticking away the moments that make up a dull day, fritter and waste the hours in an offhand way, kicking around on a piece of ground in your home town, waiting for someone or something to show you the way."

All our efforts are focussed on the 'something' that is going to change everything, whilst silently beaming out cries from the heart for genuine change, and a sense that we would like some control back please, if nobody minds.

As if by magic this book has appeared in your life, I have made and heard your pleas, suffered myself and felt your pains. On a collective level there is a lot of pain on Earth, and that needs to be transmuted into love, and this can be done, we just need more people to find the answer. You want to know the answer don't you? I know you do, you do don't you? Come on, out with it, do you want to know or not?

OK then, are you ready? The answer is simply that the world that you experience without your Human Energy Field (or H.E.F.) being activated and connected is upside down and quite possibly the wrong way round. Right here and now you are *not* the sum total of your pain and experiences! Nope, not at all, you are actually the other way around. Confused? You soon won't be.

You are more correctly the result of all your negative thoughts and feelings that have attracted negative or, at best, so-so experiences into your life. Thus compounding negative inner beliefs, like 'life is a pile of poop', or, 'I just knew that would happen to me,' or the real doozy, 'that's just my luck!' These thoughts spell trouble because they are just not true, in truth they are the result of previous negative events. By feeling these negative statements inside, we create an outer experience that is as negative as the thoughts themselves. What can the universe do except to reflect back to you more of what you mistakenly believe is your real feeling?

Here and now you are not your true self, you are a construct of all the negative feelings, thoughts and reactions that have brought you to this point in time.

How has this happened you ask, and how could you not be you? It has happened because you haven't been educated to practise the energy way and develop your Human Energy Field. You haven't been shown how energy really works in this world, how all our human faculties, higher and lower, come from energy

9

first, and not the brain, the mind, or the body.

You are not the 'you' that is really 'you' because your H.E.F. is not fixed and fully-functioning yet. It will be, but not quite yet. How could you have known this, nothing in your education has prepared you for it? There are of course people that meditate, and Yoga that stretches you, and Pilates. There are Martial Arts that can strengthen you physically and mentally. The Eastern arts tell us about Chi energy, and Chinese Acupuncture is entirely based on the energy meridians that flow up, down and around the subtle body.

Yet none of these arts advise us on how this subtle energy affects our lives and how to practically use that knowledge in our day to day experiences. Most of the reference books seem somewhat arcane and hard to understand, and not much use when someone steals your parking place at Sainsbury's. Many spiritual writers have grappled with the higher concepts, paths and ways of the Eastern sages, in an attempt to bring their knowledge into the Western world. They are braver than I am, in truth I have learned that simple is best, and basic is even better, it's the only way that I can understand things.

Put it this way: Which of the following explanations seems easier for you to grasp and digest?

"As part of the higher flow and as a result of many interactions on different levels, and indeed resulting from the actions of many lifetimes, which has brought you to a higher understanding and knowledge of the need for guilt, then transcendence through the love of all humanity, then absolving all from blame which allows the innocence of all and the joy of the universe to flow. Parking itself is a metaphor for the insertion of our joyous Merkaba into the sea of souls."

Or,

"Forgive the ingrate that stole your parking spot, do not react and do move on, another place will be better and available now."

I thought so, me too. That is what this book is about, and it's what I am about too, on a universal and energy level I'm taking Nouvelle Cuisine at the Chateau Chapelle back to Fish, Chips and gravy in newspaper, on a bench at the seaside, yummy.

I must be clear here that I completely admire and adore the great spiritual energy work writers; in fact it would be true to say that I would not be here writing this if I hadn't read and learned from the greats, and I am a devotee of their works. My point is that I read them whilst I was working with a great spiritual teacher, Hazel Raven, so if I came up against anything that I didn't understand all I had to do was to ask Hazel the next day. Not only did I get the answers, she would illustrate them with practical energy examples and explain how to incorporate them into my life. She is, and always will remain, one of my greatest blessings. She also taught me how to be practical with energy work, and how to control my own H.E.F. after it was fixed.

Hence I would like to share these methods and the associated knowledge with you, and to give you the same head start in understanding your H.E.F. that I had. Consider this book an essential crammer before you start on your greater spiritual path.

Before we can start to talk about and heal your H.E.F. we have to talk about two vital connections and the actual function and need for a H.E.F in the first place. The problems that happen repeatedly in our lives are caused by the same problems in our H.E.F's. So how do we begin to fix them? Most people that have broken H.E.F.'s are missing two connections. These connections come from the two major sources of higher energy that are available freely to us down here on Earth. They are;

1) The many-layered matrix of high frequency energy that surrounds us all; it is called by some the God-Force, by others The Matrix, and others the Morph. It is also called the Source. It is above us, around us, and if we allow it, within us. It has intelligence and compassion and a never-ending desire to share with us, and for us to benefit from its higher-frequencies. What it doesn't have are human emotions and emotional reactions. It doesn't respond to 'need' for instance. If we reject it, or do not attempt to re-connect to it, then it retreats and waits patiently until 'we' change our minds about it. I just call it 'energy' simply because it is in, or around everything that we know on Earth. In a fixed and functioning H.E.F. high-frequency energy mainly joins us through the top of our energy fields and then progresses down through the various energy centres until we are charged up, and then any excess is passed down into the Earth matrix.

2) The second connection that is vital for top-notch human function is the Earth energy. The Earth's magnetic field is a much lower frequency than higher energy, but it is just as vital that we can bring that energy up from the Earth into the base centre of our H.E.F.'s; when spiritual writers talk about being 'grounded', this is what they mean. Equally, when they talk about being 'centred', they are referring to the two vital energies being matched and equal within the H.E.F. I will talk more about these energies later on in this book.

We have to have a through flow of both these energies to really live a happy and fulfilled life, and one that is of service to the rest of humanity. One of our highest purposes on Earth is to be a 'transformer' for the higher source energy and bring it down through squeaky-clean energy fields into the Earth's matrix. Thus feeding Mother Earth the high frequencies she needs to heal the damage all our violence and explosions have caused.

Without these two connections we cannot heal our H.E.F.'s, indeed we are stranded in a silent, colourless world of ego and sensual needs that have to be satisfied, and then again, and then again. Repeat until you are completely cream-crackered! This puts us into a constant state of waiting for something to happen, of hoping for an answer. It's like we are stood buck-naked in the shower and staring at the head, waiting for the water to come, and waiting, and waiting... But until we take some action, and *reach for the tap*, nothing happens. You've got to reach for the tap and turn it on *yourself!* So come on, reach for the tap with me, and shout it out loud,

"I'm reaching for the tap!"

It's that simple, dirt simple. Come with me now and I will show you how your H.E.F. actually works, and how you can fix all your pipes and get that fabulous flow going.

Two things you need to know before I go on to describe more about your H.E.F.

1) *Everything is Energy.*

2) *The last place anything happens is in the physical third dimension.*

It's all very well me telling you all about your H.E.F and what it does; now I need to explain a little about how it does what it does, which is act as the interface between your physical body and subtle energy into the higher frequency planes where your soul resides. It does this through the opening and closing of a set of energy conduits that are called chakras.

I'm not going to go into deep discussions about your chakras, there are many other books that are solely devoted to them and go into them in great depth. Should you wish to carry this study further I will list some books at the back of this one that I consider very worthy.

To simplify the description and make it easier to understand the workings of the chakras, I have decided to depict them as four 'energy centres' rather than the traditional seven different chakras. This will help you to relate what happens in and around these centres to your daily life in a more practical manner, rather than struggling with arcane and ancient descriptions on top of everything else.

Basically the chakras extend outward from the body at right-angles to the floor. They are trumpet-shaped and can fold in as well as extend. They also extend out from the back of the body. The Crown chakra points up and out, and the base chakra points down between our legs. There are other chakras and meridians and other subtle bodies, but for the sake of simplicity and to give you a good grasp of the general workings of the H.E.F. I have chosen to leave them out of this practical guide.

My descriptions will allow you to understand more clearly that the way we translate higher energy into emotions and feelings. The energy that we encounter both shapes and colours the way that we perceive the world and this is all done through the feeling-centres, or chakras. In all my descriptions I am assuming that the chakras are all fully functioning and well. I will describe what can happen when they are damaged or dysfunctional later in the book.

The Creation Centre.

At the top of our energy fields above our heads and pointing up is the Crown Chakra, this brings down higher frequency energy for us to process into our lives. Slightly above and between our eyes is the Third-Eye chakra. Through this chakra we interpret energy that is at the level of thought and we ourselves can project thoughts out through it. At the highest level we transmit manifesting energy through here. I call these two chakras the creation centre.

To manifest our desires we pull higher energy down through the crown, then down through the rest of the H.E.F. and then back up to the third-eye and out into the universe. In energy terms this brings our desires back to us. This is in ideal circumstances with all other chakras working properly and cleared. When short -circuited the crown chakra closes and cuts off the supply of higher energy, this leaves the third eye with no option other than to process the world on the simple level of thought. So very little actual creation of desires is happening, but there will be plenty of thought about those desires.

This leaves the energy that is re-circulated for creation purposes floating around doing nothing. This causes pressure around the third-eye and can cause headaches, ear-aches and such. Because there is no operating higher connection through the crown, any excess here is projected as thoughts that are tainted with the emotion of lack, or loss, or 'have-not'. Others in the same situation project their lack as 'angry' thoughts too; you can see a reflection of the energy-reality of this in the term 'browbeating,' or 'browbeaten,' or "she was given a look that beat her down."

I often think the TV character Dr Who has crown chakra problems, because he is often inexplicably angry and hyperactive, and all his solutions to the dire problems of the universe are intellectual but laced with anger. I think I should have a word with him, and as for his relationships....?!

The Feeling Centre.

Next down the H.E.F. are the throat chakra and the heart chakra. They are life-vital chakras and I call them the feeling centre.

The throat chakra is always the weakest chakra in people that haven't done any energy work, yet it is a vital link that needs to be built up and protected. Its describing word is 'truth,' or more accurately 'facing or speaking your truth.'

Emotional energy from the heart chakra that we refuse to

process lodges here, we feel 'a lump in the throat.' When we don't want to or can't say something because we have been put on the spot, we get a 'frog in our throat.' All these energy effects are signals to work in this area of our lives. Coughs and colds show that we are too much in the head; we can't or won't get down into our heart chakras.

I must also mention that if the throat chakra is closed then you are out of here pronto, finito benito. At the rear of the throat chakra is the thin silver cord that connects our astral body with our physical. If this is severed then the result is lights out immediately.

The heart chakra is where we feel and express the highest frequency energy of all, and that is Love. The heart chakra has twin chambers, or levels, and it is easily damaged. It has a very high capacity for absorbing emotional pain that we haven't processed properly. Once filled to capacity real physical problems will ensue; poor circulation, actual heart problems, depression, lack of energy for life.

The heart chakra, like the physical heart, is the pump that circulates high- frequency energy and if it is blocked then circulation problems will begin. When this chakra becomes damaged then it can also have a knock-on effect with chakras above and below as they do not receive the higher energy or the healing earth energies. Damage here also causes premature ageing, not just of the body, but of the mind and the soul.

We must feel and process love properly in this chakra before we can give it or receive it. Any damage here also reflects in our ability to give or receive anything, we cannot give what isn't already in our heart chakras.

I was once speaking to a lady about energy work, and she asked me what came across from her, it was a genuine question so I immediately looked at her heart chakra. You know what's coming don't you? The pain from her chakra was palpable and intense, but she was a beautiful lady with an ample bosom and a low-cut t-shirt! I instantly did my best beetroot impression and looked away 'ahem-ing' nicely. Her eyes never flickered as she waited for my answer. So I said, "The stored pain in your heart is really a problem, which needs to be sorted first." Her eyes glazed over as she said, "I came in here not believing in this stuff, what you said is too close to the truth. Next time just stare at my breasts please!" With that she turned away and I never saw her again. A cautionary tale, maybe, but I reckon it's more a measure of how real heart chakra pain can be.

The Physical Self Centre.

Next down the H.E.F. we arrive at the area just above the belly-button, the solar-plexus chakra, and just below that, in the obvious area, the sacral, or sexual chakra. In energy terms this centre is where we experience the physical self, the individuation and the shaping of our characters.

The solar-plexus area in physical terms and in energy terms is where we process 'food' and energy for the continued survival of the energy and physical bodies. Blocks here show more obviously as over or underweight. Negative energy stored here can cause any number of gastric and self-esteem problems.

When our perceptions are skewed and we have problems with self-worth this is where we store them. Too much energy here, that isn't circulated, can result in too much self-esteem and arrogant or even violent behaviour. In energy terms these are all survival issues, so we are projecting and experiencing fear of our survival every time we indulge in these behaviours. If we do not like what we see of the world we close this centre down and become small and reclusive and reside in a 'broken-heart' or an overactive mind. If we are angry at the world, too much solar-plexus energy will rapidly build a flesh barrier that 'pushes' the world away, and no amount of diets will fix this until the chakra is fixed or cleared. Self-worth and individuation need to be balanced for a healthy life, and this chakra is all about balance.

The sacral chakra is not just to do with sexuality, though it is that. The sacral chakra is also about the creative force of the spark of life itself in women, and producing the catalyst of that spark in men. It also deals with the destructive force of humans as well. It receives life-generating force and it then receives a soul-spark and grows life in a physical body.

Pure light-driven high frequency creativity is from here and must be expressed. Many addictions are the result of creative impulses that have gathered here and not been used. The flip-side of the sacral is that when not expressed, or it is blocked or damaged, then our thoughts and feelings will revert to physical expression, and repeat them again and again. This can take the form of physical or verbal aggression, abusive violence or self-hatred, bigotry and race hatred, abrogation of responsibility for one's own children and their growth, overactive sexuality or even repugnance and rejection of sexuality. This is a powerful chakra that is imperative it *must* be processed.

When these two chakras are fixed and working properly, we will be supplied with an unending supply of creativity and abundance, we would have absolutely no doubts about who we are or where we want to be.

The Survival Centre.

The last and lowest of the chakras, if we're standing up, is the base chakra, the survival centre. Down there between our thighs and pointing down into the Earth is the base chakra. It is where we complete the cycle of bringing spiritual high-frequency energy spiralling down into the third physical dimension and healing the magnetic field and the subtle energies of the Earth herself.

We also use this chakra to bring spiralling-up the earthy frequencies that ground us in our body whilst maintaining the higher connection. These energies help to heal us and stabilise us on the planet. If this connection is damaged or lost we tend to drift into pure survival issues, the whole world is a threat to us and our immediate families, or formal groupings. We feel that we are right, and that we must fight the rest of the world, or our named opponents for the survival of ourselves. These thoughts are usually tempered with real panic and fear leading to anxiety attacks or worse.

This is the place where the shadow-self lives, and if this goes unprocessed and without the base connection to drain the worst of us away, then we slowly become the shadow-self, which turns us into fear-based and fear-projecting mechanisms. We live with and become the irrational, ill-considered and base thoughts and actions that are all here; dreadful acts that we all pale at, and I will not name, often ensue, with tragic results.

We have to face the fact that at the same time that we need to be grounded we must also process the darker side of ourselves, the shadow-self. It must be befriended and shown that its survival fears are irrational, lest we be consumed by its rampant ego. If we re-connect to the Earth, the healing power of this energy will connect with the energy of the sacral chakra and start to bring us back to a healthy life, and healthy thoughts and feelings.

This concludes my short run through the feeling centres and their chakras. In the next section I am going to talk about some of the influences that affect us externally, and I will conclude this chapter with a short description of negative energy and how it affects our H.E.F.'s.

There are also external influences that can damage and harass our energy fields; there is a lot of interference from electrical systems, outside cables and pylons, microwaves domestic and transmitted, mobile phones. Loud and clashing noises jangle us and crowds of people tend to lower our resistance to negative energy. There is a lot of negative frequency blasting straight at us through our TV screens, and also our computer monitors. We are not immune to the energy effects of negative events because we are passively watching them.

Obviously our modern world tends to revolve around or include all of the above, so a sense of balance is required. We can't just expel all these things from our lives, and indeed most are very useful devices, so compromise is needed, use them when we need them, but not too much.

When your H.E.F becomes blocked or damaged,then the subtle senses that energy uses, such as intuition, purpose or intent, are also clouded and in some cases removed from us altogether. It's harder for us to make choices that belong to a higher purpose when we can't access that energy. They seem somehow less relevant than the in-your-face events of the humdrum world. We return to just mental 'thinking' and decision making that is based on the past and the future, and not the 'real' subtle feelings of the 'now'.

People that cannot sense the subtle energy and are blocked from this by the damage in their own energy fields will often believe that subtle energy doesn't exist. Their ego will not allow them to admit the existence of something that they cannot sense. There is a tragic-comic and deeply ironic quality to this denial that is hard for them to deal with properly. The very thing that they need help with, their damaged H.E.F., is the very knowledge that they deny and sometimes, quite vehemently, push away.

I feel the saddest when I come across somebody with no H.E.F., the damage, abuse and self-abuse has become so bad that their fields have collapsed in on them, and their chakras have stopped completely. They have absolutely no protection against negativity and no connection to higher energy, they become very prone to illness, damage, and other kinds of abuse. They become totally ruled by ego and feel the world as a great pressure or as something that should serve them. Famous people that crash and burn almost always have collapsed or no H.E.F.'s, it's amazing just how many of the 'beautiful people' have little or no energy signature beyond the low-frequency basal energy of the ego.

They are depleting all their bodies' higher resources as they run down to inevitable collapse entirely on nervous energy and mental thought energy.

Of course there is always the hope of rescue and reconnection, but they have to start somewhere, they have to admit to themselves the existence of what they haven't got, and to realise, that in many cases, money just can't buy it back. Whether we know it or not, we are always 'in control' of our lives, the lack of energy in our lives merely points out that we have switched our choices over to the circle world.

All we need to do is stop thinking and start feeling, but as you know by now, you have to start somewhere, and that where is here and now.

Chapter Two

Emotions and their reflections.

A good question right now might be, "How do you feel?" You may respond truthfully, and your answer would reflect what was going on in your life, and it would be wrong. Why do I say that? Because what is going on now is the 'reflection' of the thoughts and feelings that you have projected out into the world through your H.E.F., and if you are reading this I can cheekily assume that you need at least a little work doing.

I know that this concept is a little difficult to get a hold of in the beginning; it certainly fooled me for ages. I mean how can our feelings not describe who we are, and surely we are our feelings? Well, we would be our feelings if our H.E.F's were working perfectly, if we were transmitting the truth of our souls through a functioning energy field. Until we are in that great state then we are a muddled- up mess of all our reactions to the events that have happened so far, and those events are a result of all the previous thoughts and feelings that we have had, phew!

The beginnings of this confused state are always related to a damaged or disconnected energy field. The universe itself is designed as a huge interconnected reflecting system. It gives to us what we ask from it; with a working and connected H.E.F. then what we project, or 'ask' for, is what we will receive, more or less, depending on the accuracy and focus of our thoughts and feelings. So what we get back is in the realms of higher energy and to do with our authentic selves. If, on the other hand, we are not projecting what we desire, but because our energy field is damaged, we are simply reacting emotionally to the events that come to us. Then all we get is that energy reflected back, tainted with the emotion that we projected previously.

This creates a negative loop of energy inside our H.E.F. that doesn't connect to higher energy or drain through the Earth connection. The only place left for it to go is to be projected outside of us. So we hurl all the frustration and anger out into the universe, silently fulminating and raging, mistakenly 'thinking' that this is OK because nobody is a mind-reader, right? Wrong, what happens is that package of energy hurtles at the intended parties or party and impacts their energy fields. This packet of energy is noted by the universe and the 'speed' of your energy is noted. So some time after, when you have calmed down and forgotten this little episode, you are sitting quietly, and the phone rings, a negative event occurs, and this throws you into another emotional state, the cat's come back.

What you don't see is that the new negative event is the earlier package being returned to you in kind, exactly the same as you sent it out, but happening at a different time and maybe to different people, but always including you. So the new reaction is sent out to create another negative event, and so it continues. It isn't possible to be on Earth and do nothing, I don't mean activities here, I mean without us being involved in the energy of where we are right now.

Human beings are energy generators, most are never still or mentally quiet unless they are asleep, and even then they are involved in dreaming. That is one of the reasons that it is very important to get connected to the higher energy and to start getting jiggy with it! Energy never stops, and the higher the frequency we can get ours too, then the better it is for us and for all around us, and that includes loved ones and friends.

The realm of the 'tick-tock' is entirely run on the two tenets of ego and being reactive. The act of doing that connects the two is thought, but not 'feeling' thought that has meaning and significance, no, I mean the trivial thought that we are taught to experience. From birth we are filled with images of war and chaos and examples of other people being horrible and violent to each other, and the helplessness of us all, and our inability to change 'how things are'. We are told to fit in and be a useful member of society, at no time are we told that we have the capability of changing our lives by changing how we think and feel. So realistically, it's a rare person that breaks the mould and starts to think for his or her self. Go easy on yourself about this, the 'you-can't-do-anything-else-about-this' energy loop of the circle world is very powerful indeed.

The 'reactive' mind is the product of this world, and let's be honest, it's exactly where the controllers desire us to be. Maybe they don't know any better because it's what they've been taught? How can anybody find out about their H.E.F.? It certainly isn't going to be on the news, nor will the newspapers print it. You can imagine the headline; "Film at eleven, lots of people are happy with their new energy fields and are being nice to each other!" It isn't going to happen is it? It would be good if it did though.

Ego is the construct that the human brain builds when it has no reference to higher energy, because it has a dysfunctional energy field. Ego can only refer to self and then project that outward; it cannot take any responsibility for itself. It is a wayward child that has hijacked the soul-centres of many millions of people. But they have allowed this because ego is also a coping mechanism that lets us function in a world, that we are told, just isn't fair. It is pointless to rage and rail against ego running the circle world because that is its M.O.! It doesn't work to get angry or huffy about not being taught about the H.E.F. because that is the way that the circle world operates; get furious and rage against that which you can't change and you slot yourself neatly into the loop. You will become like the shiny silver ball in a pinball machine slapped from pillar to post, and someone else is benefitting from your high score! Cut yourself a lot of slack and don't react about it, instead decide to redress the imbalance and find out more about your H.E.F., gently intend to yourself that you will find the time to finish this book, whatever your ego says.

Let's look at some emotions and how they affect your H.E.F. By the way, Wayne Dyer has a great tag for emotions, he calls them 'energy in motion, e-motion' superb. Most of the many random thoughts that flitter across our consciousness are not our own, they come from many sources, including the people around us, and especially the TV. Emotions, more specifically anger and feelings of aggression, work in the same fashion. They can leech across to us from other people's energy, or they can be projected at us from another person. Say a boss at work lets rip at us verbally for no good reason; we can't answer back for fear of our jobs, so we travel home having a rubbish journey, and later at home we vent this anger at spouse or the kids.

In energy terms the anger attack would have impacted us in the third eye chakra and the solar-plexus chakra. Because the energy field can't bring down higher-energy to dilute the anger or drain it to earth for cleansing, the bolt of energy circulates through our e-fields until we can vent it, or more accurately, project it at someone else.

Even though the event has ended, the energy has not dissipated, and we feel this expressed inside us as anger and humiliation. Even venting it by ranting about the boss to a friend or partner involves them in the energy loop. It also makes our energy set-up more aggressive, and we would be far less likely to find a positive event to cheer us up, in fact the universe would move quickly to validate our negative feelings.

If we suddenly and randomly feel aggressive or angry for no apparent reason, then it is likely that someone nearby has projected that at us, or we have just walked through a cloud of negative energy that was created earlier. Maybe someone had an argument there, or even worse. With no way to channel away this energy then that taint and the feeling of disquiet will stay with us. There is nowhere else for it to go, that is until we project it at somebody or something later. If we don't do that, then a taint of that disquiet will stay with us until it slowly dissipates. Even if the energies that we come across during the day are of small magnitudes, it doesn't take long for the cumulative effect to make us feel miserable or moody, and we reach out for something to cheer us up.

The problem is that we have become used to energy patterns that fit the way we live in the circle world. We actually accept things that upset us or make us angry with a fatalistic shrug, as though this were a punishment from an angry deity. We never think to change the pattern because we think that the pattern 'is' our life, rather than a negative energy thought pattern, or recording, that we keep playing again and again.

Each and every day we come across things that trigger the negative ways that we feel, and in the ego-ruled circle world manner, we react to life's apparent misfortunes. It could be a song that reminds us of an old relationship; we listen intently and it seems fun at first. Then because we are giving emotional attention to these old feelings we actually re-activate that person in our damaged H.E.F.; we become the person that we were years before, with the same fears. Problem is that this is layered on top of what we are going through today! Nostalgia definitely ain't what it used to be, it affects us now!

It's the same with smells and tastes of favourite foods, we could be on a diet, and it won't work. Why? Because we think we need willpower, but what we actually need is to let go of an energy pattern that no longer suits us. We walk past the shop and smell or see the food or whatever it is, can we resist it, no way, the ego is going to find a way to get that item and it's going to justify it to you too. The ego can't see the good in dropping the pattern, because all it exists from are patterns of behaviour. Ego is a jukebox with a number of tunes in it that aren't variable, it can only play those tunes, or act out those same energy patterns. Suggesting to ego that it change its tunes for better ones is pointless, ego cannot see past its metaphoric nose.

However many times we intend or make a pact or start a diet, we are going to keep blowing those deadlines or waistlines until we actually make the effort to connect to higher energy and clear out the useless patterns of ego from our H.E.F. and chakras. It really is the only way.

This is why 'emotion' or feeling 'emotional' is not real feeling, it is in fact a weaker 'catch-all' expression that describes the many ways in which anger and fear and disappointment rock and roll through our chakras and in the process weaken us, whilst appearing to be authentic. It is difficult to feel the truth of real feelings without some serious inner-exploration, no not that kind, I mean sitting quietly and wondering what all this rubbish going on in your head is all about. The only purpose most thought has is to cloud important issues and keep you from finding true feeling.

Remember what Bruce Lee says to his young student at the beginning of his most famous film *Enter the Dragon*; "Don't think, feel, I want to see real emotional content." Spoken by a true energy master and I wouldn't have argued with him, would you?

Having said that I must allow that getting to 'real emotional content' in the circle world is a journey in itself. We are so used to the dampening and smothering energy of disappointments and reading/watching dreadful things happening all over the globe, that maintaining any happiness of our own seems like a bridge too far. But whenever we do touch higher energy we get a feeling of excitement that is hard to place, it feels like an anticipation of something that is 'going' to happen, we don't know 'what' or 'where' but we know that something good will happen.

This is a real connection to higher energy and we all know this feeling, it has happened to all of us at some time, even the most concertedly miserable types. We actually chase this feeling hoping to replicate it with an emotional leaning forward that we call yearning. When this doesn't work we start to substitute in the human-created substitutes like food, sugar, alcohol, nicotine, etc.

Most of us mean well, and don't intend to become addicted to anything, but we can't see another way to get to that feeling. This is part of the problem of a disconnected H.E.F., but there is another slight hitch too; what we are doing when we yearn is to project our hopes and feelings into a 'future' time, when we actually want it to happen now. We can't see it happening now because of the blocking effect of low-frequency energy in our H.E.F's, so we push it forward. We are sitting here and now, unhappy and yearning and imagining our future as better. This is a simple contradiction that has far-reaching effects. It leaves us in a state of stasis, in an energy loop that has to disappoint us. We become beings that have every capability to manifest what we desire, that are sitting and waiting, doing more and doing more, still waiting for the good to come.

So, how do we get to this real feeling? Well, as a start to the answer let's have a look at what we call our 'character'. We come through childhood into teenage and then adulthood, exchanging many energies and events with family and friends, and increasingly as we grow, a wider group of people. In this circle world not many of us complete this journey knowing about our H.E.F's and using meditation and quiet, do we? So we haven't had much opportunity to balance our selves using the higher energy connection and the healing Earth connections have we? There has to be something that we become though, and we search through all our reactions to previous experiences and build a construct of those events and their associated feelings, positive or negative.

The layers and layers of these energy constructs that we mistakenly call 'character' are always made up of emotional reactive memories that we 'think' we remember, but are actually clumps of energy that are part of our H.E.F. In the ego- ruled circle world life is depicted as a long sequence of events through time that are 'done to' and 'happen to' us. Rather than a chosen sequence of desires that mesh beautifully with each other, this is how it should be.

OK nobody is perfect, not even me, and so we all arrive here with some 'stuff' that we are going to have to sort out at some time in our lives. Point is that life would be a lot easier for all of us if we were told that all our reactions are just that; emotional reactions to projected energy that contains packets of negative feeling that we readily add to our own collection of negative feelings. We call this 'growing-up' and put it down to experience. This is typical of an ego-ruled world, where we are expected to deal with these hard times and then effortlessly stand aside. Trouble is that it isn't as easy as that, as we all know, and this energy and the bad feelings are all too real, and they impact on our lives, causing us to take-in and then project outwards whatever that energy is.

We don't know about these energy exchanges because we have never been taught about them, how can we hope to understand low-frequency energy if we are not told what it is? How can we deal with a sudden feeling of anger or depression, or a headache from nowhere, if we don't know where they are from? Short of reaching for the pharmaceuticals we can't, so the energy is added to the collective energy that we call character. And all of this is without ever having connected to higher energy or the healing Earth energies in any way at all. The whole thing seems bleak doesn't it, but that is exactly where this planet is at right now. OK there are many more people than before searching for more answers and spiritual solutions, but many more are needed.

Before we can begin to look at unravelling all these intricate layers of events and reactions to get to the core of us as human beings with an immortal soul living a physical life, I'll have to talk about another confusing emotional issue that affects a lot of us, and that is infatuation, or obsession.

We are simple beings that are forced to reach for greater

complications in our lives. This happens because we all have an inner knowing, a knowing feeling that there is more to life than is presented to us. We aren't sure what 'it' is, but we will ardently search for it so we look for the deepest feelings we can find, love and relationships. What we don't know yet is that the real answer is higher energy and our glorious re-connection, but that doesn't stop us searching.

If I had my way I'd say don't bother falling in love until you sort out your higher and earth connections, but that just isn't going to happen, I know. Truth is that love and relationships are what have saved us from far worse things happening than are now. Even the lowliest of us will naturally search and seek out kinship and friendship, that feeling of belonging to something or somebody that we all crave to some degree or other. On the positive side this is where our small redemptions lie, where we define our being-ness.

Why then, if love and belonging and relationships are paramount and our highest expression (so far), do we have divorce, pre-nups, family bust-ups, wedding disasters, love triangles, and so forth? I'd like to suggest that it is because we have a 'mental' idealised picture of what love and relationships should be, and that the actuality of it is that 'love' is based on infatuation and projected energy. Stories, films and TV fill us with the idea that love and living together should be Shambala in the bedroom, Nirvana in the kitchen and so forth; the actual human reality will often fall short.

When we agree to live with someone we also make an energy agreement that our H.E.F.'s will mesh and we will be one. If only it was that simple, but it isn't, we are complex energy creatures, and without higher energy and healing earth connections, we aren't quite balanced yet. When we meet and conjoin, we quite literally plug-in to each others' H.E.F.'s, whatever they may contain. On a human level we may have convinced ourselves that this other human is our twin-soul and that this was meant to be, that the other person completes us, that finally we have found each other. Sadly, these are danger signs, warnings of infatuation, and with infatuation trouble soon follows. Prince Charming quickly turns into Shrek; Cinderella becomes the wicked Step-mother. When things go wrong we move away from the inner-warmth back to the outer projections of the circle-world; shouting and arguments are followed by affairs and then acrimonious splits. But this person was everything to you, wasn't she/he?

What is happening here, why has beautiful infatuation failed us? It is because we attract to ourselves the events that mirror the energy in our H.E.F.'s, and this also include people? So the people we attract or are attracted to seem to be the people we are 'drawn to' or we 'fancy', i.e. they tick of all the requirements on our inner 'wish' list. What we don't realise is that the inner list is coloured and influenced by the energy and the reactive memories that remain in our chakras. So we are actually attracting the people that mirror the energy that we are projecting, they are the people that match our energy and they come to help us sort out those problems.

This is not always the desired scenario especially if the answer to those negative energy signatures is touching our inner pain. Yes love can and will ease our pain, but we need to connect at both ends of our H.E.F. for that healing to be permanent, and not just another run around the block with an old and familiar negative emotional pattern.

Once you consent to a relationship you also consent to the mutual exchange of energies between your H.E.F.'s. Let's say that you have done some soul-searching and managed to raise the frequency of your energy, giving yourself the space to allow someone in your life. But because you haven't re-connected yet you still have some 'self-worth' energy issues floating about you. Along comes what seems to be Mr or Miss Perfect. They have no self-worth issues but loads of other issues, real baggage. You are pulled by the feeling that their confidence will help you and you will heal together.

Not quite, what happens is your energy will take a severe battering and draining, think of it like this: Two cars are sitting next to each other, one with a flat battery and it won't start. The other has a strong battery and can help the non-starter. The batteries are connected by cable, what happens? Can the other car start? No it can't, and why? Because when two batteries are connected they equalise, the low takes from the high power, and they both become low power and neither can now start.

What should have happened is that the strong car protects itself by having the engine running and thus protecting the energy charge in the battery. Thus it would have stayed charged and the low car would have started and had a chance to recharge. Think of the engine running as your H.E.F. being connected at both ends, higher and healing energy, and this is exactly how it works. No matter how good both people's intentions, the pair will drain and be drained, again and again, repeating the same energy patterns again and again, until at least one of them re-connects.

If one re-connects and the other doesn't, then as their connection increases they will begin to resent being drained and will drift further apart. Also, being connected reduces the need for the ego to be part of your life, whilst when somebody is losing an energy connection that has been feeding them, then their ego will kick in even stronger in its apparent struggle for survival.

If we rely on a person to be our rock, our strength, then we have invested emotional energy into that person, and if they aren't connected then it is very unlikely that we will ever see a dividend. More often they will require more and more investment, always with the promise of future improvement. If you are considering the path of energy and fixing your H.E.F. first you must look at your relationships honestly and ask yourself if you actually trust you to rely on you, and not the rescuing powers of partners or family and friends.

If you maintain a positive energy connection then relying on others will become an appreciative love, and will transmute into you giving freely, which for them is a great gift and helps you too. If in your search for love you lean on friends or family too much they will resent this and back away, you will become a drain upon those you love. Backing away and beginning to trust yourself to cope with things is a powerful signal of your desire to re-connect to your H.E.F.

The reverse can happen if you are a giving person, and you give of yourself too much to another. Eventually the other will see you in a kind of messianic glow and realise that they can't possibly match you, or return your gifts in kind. Contrary to your intentions they will see themselves in a poorer light and their ego will begin to class you as trouble. At first they will seem ungrateful and reticent, and then if you persist, they will become truculent and maybe even terminate the relationship. Backing away gracefully is the answer here too, except this time you have to trust that they will find their own way forward; you just have to let them go with love.

If and when you decide to rebuild your connections, then there is something else that I would be careful of, and that is meeting old flames, especially if you hope to rekindle the flames with your new-found spiritual power. It might not be as easy as you think, even though you will enjoy the initial ease of the conversation and start to entertain the idea that this could develop again. The basic problem will be that they will have no idea who you are now, after your re-connection you will have lost a lot of the very energy patterns that kept you together, so even though you have intimate knowledge of them and appear to have the upper hand, you have improved. What if the other thinks that they have made progress but haven't really done much at all? Will you tell them? I wouldn't.

Why? Because they will be firing packets of energy at you that are part of the old you, expecting responses that are the old you. Sooner or later they will notice that you are not responding in the 'old' way and the projections get stronger. Unless you make your 'farewells' and 'au revoirs' very quickly, then those energy packets will start to cut off your new connections and you will morph back into the old you, but still with no chance of progression because the disgruntled ex-partner will think you have 'changed'.

Let me show you the power of these exchanges without you having to move from where you are now. It's quite easy to show you just how powerful emotional energy is.

Begin by relaxing in an armchair or somewhere that you are comfortable. Take a few long and deep breaths and empty your mind of all the chattering thoughts and day to day energy. Choose an event from your past that has real emotional significance to you, try and make it a positive one because we don't want to awaken any old and unused energy patterns here. This is better without any interruptions, so don't have music in the background, you need to be with yourself for this. Relax all your muscles and breathe deeply, now close your eyes and begin to recall the occasion. Build the picture of it strongly in your minds-eye. Hear people speaking and listen to the tones of the emotion in their voices, hear their breath, and look closely at them. Are there any smells, can you pick them out, where you eating, call that taste back into your mouth. Were you excited, where you running, jumping? If you were at a gig call it back, all the people, and the noise. Take as long as you need and run the whole thing through.

I bet that you just opened your eyes with a 'wow!' If you were excited , then your heart will be beating faster, there could be other physical signs, is your skin sweating, do you feel the changes in energy around your skin, heat changes and flows of the tingles? Even if this is the first time that you have tried that visualisation you will feel something, I am sure of that.

However intense and real it seemed, it wasn't; you have just felt the power of subtle energy and how it brings that energy memory pattern back to you as faithfully as watching a DVD on the TV. Scientists and Doctors will say that it is the power of the imagination alone and the mind playing tricks. But the energy is in the physical effects, you weren't there and nothing has happened really, yet it seemed so real. At your command the emotional energy replayed the physical event in your minds-eye. That is the power of subtle energy. That is the very real power of emotional energy.

There are many other examples of the ways that emotional energy plays out in our lives; in this chapter I have chosen to illustrate just a few of the more powerful ones. Energy that isn't connected to source and to earth will always be played out in our lives as a drama. Until we re-connect there is no way that we can avoid that, and in a way that is very apt, because the ego-driven circle world is all about dramas. We have become so conditioned to this state of being that we expect it, and we eagerly listen to others' dramas in the hope that they will be suffering as we do. This isn't a negative way to be, because in the circle world validation comes from being part of a tribe or group that have shared experiences and pain.

The most powerful aspect of grasping for and then achieving energy freedom through our H.E.F is that of individuation. We become the power of ourselves, we can connect to and be part of all things and all people, respecting them and loving them for their spiritual core and not judging them for what they do. By granting us freedom to be an individual with real spiritual self-worth and self-esteem, we escape from the circle world, and then we return because we then know that we can help, that we can give back.

All that you have to remember is that, especially with emotional energy, you have to start somewhere, and that where is here and now. Everything that you feel about your life is coloured by all the events leading up to now, until that is, you begin to reconnect with your higher-self and the higher source, and the Earth-Mother and the healing energy.

Start by accepting that you haven't always known about this energy stuff, and I know for sure that you have always made the best choices that you can in the circumstances that you have found yourself. You have to give yourself a bit of breathing space and *do not react* to this new knowledge with judgement and condemnation of yourself. Neither should you flip into denial and anger. Just be still, quiet the mind, and know that you always have had the option to re-connect and that it will never be taken away from you. Also you are free to fall back into the circle world again, should you so wish. Everything is choice, choose your H.E.F. and start by accepting yourself, relax and breathe deeply, and begin to trust yourself, you're worth it.

Chapter Three

Thoughts project.

Isn't it an incredible thing that I can sit here and type these words and you can read them and understand them, interpret their meaning and then apply them to something that you can relate to in your own life? Our eyes and brains interpret visual signals through synapses firing and then return those signals as understanding in our minds.

Well that's the theory, in my mind some things can get a bit garbled and I can misinterpret someone's tone or meaning and can get a bit miffed. We all can, at least I think so. I mean if I don't mind it doesn't matter, or does it? At least I think so, well that's food for thought, and I'll give it some thought later.

Are you lost yet? I am, and I think I might be dizzy too! What I am trying to show above is how thoughts jump about and evolve, with one following another and then triggering another, and then another... Are all these thoughts really necessary and where do they come from? Are we actually random-thought generators that have no idea what we will come up with next, lolloping about in our mental spaces like a dog chasing a football around a field? What am I thinking next? I don't know, oh! Cheesecake and rice, but I'm still angry at him, need a bath, payday Friday.

I'm being flippant but that's what happens to people that live in their minds in the circle world, they are prey to millions of random thoughts and ideas that are beamed about and projected by millions of other people. Could you count how many thoughts you have had today? No chance and how many of those are your own? Are you sure about that?

We take it as a given that our mind space is inviolate, that nobody could know what we are thinking, unless we telegraphed our feelings with facial expressions. There may be people who can read others' minds, but I am not one of them. I'm glad too; what a maelstrom of stuff we may find in there, and maybe some not so nice thoughts about ourselves or others that we know.

Maybe we are reading it wrong, could it be that things are the other way round? It is the way of the circle world, and I believe it to be so. What if it isn't a person 'reading' our thoughts that is the problem, instead, it is their thoughts being projected at us that cause us worry and stress? What if we are also subject to the mirrored reflections of our own thoughts that we have projected at others?

Let me share an example with you, I am going to show you how our reaction to life's events creates the mental/emotional morass of thoughts which in turn creates our 'real lives.' This frustrating cycle of thoughts creating the events that we then react to is the cycle of the circle world in action.

Marla has just participated in a spiritual retreat weekend; she thought that she deserved the break. She works hard and can afford to indulge herself. It's part of her new plan to actually 'do' something about it. Marla has toned with Tibetan ringing bowls, she has had aromatherapy massages whilst listening to joyful Whale song, and she has chanted her canticles from her head to her toes, and had her head Indian massaged. She came home on the Sunday night feeling amazing. She unpacked and had a hot bath with incense and candles. Once in the hot water she ran through her intentions for the coming week as her guru had told her to do. She will apply all the spiritual laws that she now knows and everything in her life will change for the better. She *will* get that promotion, her boss *will* be nice to her, her kids *will* be the best that they can be, and she *will* succeed because has intended it so.

Marla gets ready for bed happy in the knowledge that the

world *will* change for her. Even though the guru finished the retreat by telling them that this was just the beginning of their spiritual progress, Marla knows that what she feels is true and that she is healed. She feels so much better now than she has felt before, how could it not be true?

Marla awakes the next day and smiles at the morning; she is ready for the 'perfect day.' She heads down for breakfast dressed and in balance. Her youngest son spills his milky cereal over his clean uniform, no matter. The middle son upsets youngest by laughing at his plight, no matter. Eldest daughter is wearing too much make-up and giving out the usual back chat, no matter. Marla smiles and intones under her breath, "peace and calm, let them be as they are, all unfolds before me." This is the mantra that will always plug her back into the healing energies of the weekend.

Normally she would have lost her temper, but she hasn't and she silently claps herself on the back, it's a battle won, and she ignores the nagging little thought that says 'why aren't they behaving better?'

Driving to the train station and the usual slow moving traffic isn't getting to her; she just intones her mantra happily. Then just as she turns into the car park a taxi swings around in front of her without indicating. It's an illegal u-turn and he clips the front of her car. She is shocked so she stops and gets out. The taxi scoots off and she doesn't get the number. She looks around but no one else saw the incident. Her bumper is hanging off and the traffic behind beeps impatiently. As she parks the car Marla isn't feeling too good but she remembers to intone her mantra sure in the knowledge that this happened for a reason, but she's not sure what.

The train arrives; it is full, but no matter, Marla has her mantra. A young man stands uncomfortably close to her and his i-thingy is at mega volume. She intones the mantra but it keeps being interrupted as she begins to wonder about what happened with the cab, should she have got some witnesses, what will the insurance say? The noise irritates her, so she glares at the boy and shuffles away from him, he glares back and turns it up to eleven.

The train pulls into her station and she hurriedly jumps off catching a button of her jacket on the still opening door. She watches the button plummet onto the tracks below and she intones 'damn!' She glances at her watch, the train was delayed, she only has a few minutes.

Marla struggles to compose her thoughts as she walks into the office, both people that she passes nod and notice the offending button, she self-consciously covers the dangling strands of cotton. A bloom of embarrassment flares pink all over her face as she stomps into her office and slams the door behind her.

She flops into the chair thinking 'stupid mantra, useless thing, what has changed? New day, same rubbish, everything is upside down!' Her mobile phone beeps; it's a text from her friend Jenna, 'Hope you loved the weekend as much as I did, and don't forget your mantra!' Marla glares at the phone and then skims it across the desk. Stupid mantra, stupid weekend, what a waste of good money! Her secretary pops her head round the door; "Boss is on the warpath, you forgot to close the Lavenham deal when you left early on Friday!"

Marla curses silently to herself; how could she have forgotten that fifty grand deal? Stupid mantra, how could she have been suckered in so comprehensively? Nothing has changed, nothing will, well this is shaping up to be the perfect day! Whatever will be next?

Her Boss throws open the door; "This had better be good Marla....." Stupid mantra!

So what has happened to Marla, why didn't the mantra work?

Well the problem is that Marla wasn't connected to the higher energy and the healing force; she only thought that she was. She hadn't done enough to fix her H.E.F. but she *thought* that she had. Marla thought that the weekend would do the whole job in one fell swoop, after all she'd paid good money for it, and the trouble was that it didn't. It was a step, a first step, a good first step, but no more than that.

Marla *thought* that repeating the mantra would fix all the many ways that she reacted to her life and that it would undo all her previous and active thought constructs, and mend all the manifestations that they had brought. In short she *thought* that two days of physical relaxation and feeling better would be the catch-all answer to fixing up the mess of her life. Marla didn't realise that this was too tall an order for her to match up to.

All the years of wrong thinking and emotionally negative creation cannot be simply undone by a massage and a mantra, a lot more attention must be paid than that. But nobody told her that, they just bigged-up the guru and the weekend, how could it fail? How could it make things *any worse?* How indeed? The mantra could have worked over time if she paid close attention to her thought patterns and sought to fix them one at a time, it couldn't fix them all at once, nor could it produce instant results.

She enjoyed the weekend, but what it actually did was gloss over the depth of her problems and make her think that there was an easy answer and here it was right before her. She had joined the guru in intending to build a magnificent bridge from this world to the divine, but she had forgotten to stop by the builders' merchants for some bricks and mortar.

Marla reached for the sky in the form of a joyful group session and the joy of shared goals and the company of fellow spiritual people. These are all nice things but they are a distraction from the fact that real work needs to be done alone. Re-connecting is a function that restates our individuality and finds the real us from higher energy. We must start this journey by being willing to invite spirit into our lives whilst we are alone, and addressing the problems that incorrect thought has created.

There is a saying in energy talk that goes 'thoughts create.' Well yes they do, if you are coming from an H.E.F that is connected at both ends and you have worked on your chakras and have a mental outlook that is both positive and calm at the same time. Then you can freely project your desires into source energy through your third-eye chakra in the confidence that they will return with the events that you ordered. But until then we will have to chat for a while about another energy phrase.

Thoughts project and attract.

As we progress through life in the circle world, if we are coming through ego and not higher energy, then we tend to build mental constructs that we identify with and can also hide behind. I am from this town, I am this race, I am that country, I don't like that place, I am better than them, they are not my class, they think they are better than me, I'm not scum like them. You get the idea, they can be much more complicated than my examples with multiple levels of pain and justifications and why's and wherefore's. The constructs could be our pain and the awful life we've had so far, they could be others' pain projected at us that we have been subjected to there are many reasons.

They all share a common trait though; they bind us to the past and to the events that created the mental/emotional stress in the first place. If they involve family members or past lovers, or friends that have betrayed us, or stolen money from us, or maybe just battered us with unending flatulence, they all say the same thing, I am stuck in this place. I have no power, I have no choice; please free me, 'cos I am a victim.

As I mentioned earlier, these are just thoughts, they cannot hold us in one place, can they? Well yes they can, remember earlier when we did that exercise to show you the power of emotional energy? Well mental energy has the same power, it has a different flavour, but it can still hold us rooted to the spot, unable to progress or process all the wrongs and hurts that we *think* we have suffered.

It's typical of the circle world that our thoughts have become the thorns in our sides that they can be until we sort them out. What they should be is our first line of defence; they should be carefully selected and applied to fine-tune our energy fields, using their commanding qualities to direct what we want to happen in our lives. They are the method by which we monitor and understand our feelings, and the state of the 'who we are,' and the 'where we are at' side of things.

Nowhere else in our consciousness are we closer to or more aware of the divine connection to source energy of our true nature than in our thoughts. The brain should be the biochemical buddy of the full power of our mind through the H.E.F., and not just a mass of stuff inside our skulls tick-tocking away. The connection of brain to mind, and therefore thought to creation, is a gift from source energy. It is also our lifeline that is never taken away from us, like a broadband cable connection it is always on and we can access it anytime, anywhere.

Whatever the state of our emotions and condition of our physical bodies, whatever dire situations or trouble we are in, the first and last actions we will have are thoughts. Everything in our lives originates in and is a result of thoughts. Therefore it is up to us to increase the vibrations of our thoughts to a higher level, to make them kinder and wiser, and improve the people that we are.

You are in charge of your life, but only if you want to be, and are willing to start taking responsibility for the thought space that you have. Any thought time taken up with negative, judgmental or even downright nasty thoughts can only harm you in the end. The fantastic paradox of taking that control back in your life is that you do this by thinking less, not more. Replace those random roiling thoughts with peaceful ones, and angry thoughts with graceful ones, and you will begin to become a free and connected mind.

Why isn't it easier for us to do this? Why can't we just 'switch' into a better way of thinking and thus change our lives for the better? The answer lies in those pesky thought constructs that we have been living with for years; the trouble with them is that they think that they are in charge. They are so used to commanding you with those familiar negative habits and thought patterns that they don't want to let go! They gatecrashed the party, ate all your cakes and jelly, are drunk on your punch, and listen up, you invited them in!

We don't have to debate our thought patterns with others, we can stay inside the mind with hidden feelings and repressions, and we can concoct the stories that gain us the attention that we need. What the circle world doesn't tell us, though, is that at the same time that we are 'thinking' these patterns, we are also 'projecting' them outwards, first at the object of those thoughts, and then into the ethers. These thoughts are then processed and returned to us in exactly the same form, but later.

If that thought is of a person that we are disapproving of, then it impacts their H.E.F. then zaps out to be translated back to us with the same negativity. So we are hit back with the same force that we project, but at a different time. The state of our whole self is continually projected outwards until we learn to connect and then control our thoughts and H.E.F.'s. So we walk this Earth in a mire of mucky energy that we have instigated, this brings events to us that we do not like, oh no, so we project (think about) more disappointments and negativities, and then the next day we suffer more bad stuff, and on it goes.

If our H.E.F.'s aren't metaphorically coats on and buttoned up then we are also prey to the negative thoughts of others. I'm sure that we have all walked past a dodgy- looking person and had the 'shivers,' and what do we say? "Somebody just walked over my grave..." No they didn't, what happened is somebody projected subtle negative energy at you and you felt it. The reason why you felt this and not other energies is that negative and nasty thoughts are at the lowest frequencies and therefore are the easiest to detect.

For many people day to day life is made up of this negative loop of the mind created by being stuck in the mental projections of the third eye. This is predominantly 'doing' energy, so we are impelled to 'do' more stuff, whether that be buying, eating, drinking, talking, it will always be more. The brain is in charge, and as it can only 'think' and not add emotional or moral weight, we can only 'do', thus we head for a stimulus glut that can only be sated by more doing. These constant thought patterns have produced constant results in our lives that, no matter how much we dislike them, cannot be removed or resolved until we 'change our minds.'

Persistent thought patterns create persistent results in our lives.

Those pesky little nasty thoughts beggar off and are only too happy to bring back a big pile of nasty things for us to deal with, chuckling at our ignorance. The things in our lives that hassle us and we don't like very much, have to be the result of thoughts; either someone else's that we have reacted to, or our own that we have projected and have faithfully returned.

What the circle world won't say though, is that the very same process that works for the negative events and thoughts is the one that works for positive thoughts and events too. It's obvious that we need to stop these pesky interfering patterns of negative thoughts, and we are going to do that by thinking as little as possible, because we know what we have to do, we have to start somewhere.

Everything is vibration; high, low or in-between.

We are attracting to us the type of events and people that match the qualities of the thoughts that we are projecting. This has been

45

going on for as long as we have been alive and it will continue until we move into the forgiving space that will allow us to re-connect our H.E.F's and plug back into the healing energy of Mother Earth. Remember this, and allow it to sink into your mind;

The last place anything happens is on the Earth plane.

Anything that occurs in the physical third dimension was not created here; it is a resultant manifestation from the higher frequencies of source energy. It is mirrored back into the physical in exactly the same manner as it was sent out, with the same emotion, positive or negative, and the same intent, again, positive or negative. And in the words of Ella Fitzgerald, "How long has this been going on?" Look at how long you've been down here doing time on planet Earth, and that's an indication of how long you've had to practise and perfect your mental 'protection' systems that do more harm than good.

Some people have been so locked into their mental systems that they don't know what they are setting themselves up for. When so much negative third-eye projecting has happened that you can't see what good can happen to you, then you are like Cyclops in the 'X-men' with your visor full-open and firing negative mental thoughts into the world, obliterating any good that is trying to get to you.

It's often in cases like this that the projections reach a critical mass and something has to stop them. You will often find that person's higher-self working with the negative energy to get an end to the projecting. It is often better that a calamity slaps you in hospital and shuts you up for a while, than the negative damage continue in your life. Unfortunately the circle world only sees the effect of physical and emotional damage and to a certain extent mental damage; at no point does it take into account the soul-damage that all the negative mental projection can produce.

This is the territory where serious personal damage or loss can occur, through inexplicable accidents or terrible crimes, always, it appears, perpetrated on the innocents. People may lose so much of their ability to see beyond their negative thoughts that they attempt to take their own lives, a folly of monumental proportions. There is a great moment in the film 'Constantine', where John Constantine is explaining how he is damned to walk the Earth 'seeing' all the negativity and evil spirits because he was a 'suicide that survived.' A fair warning that should be heeded, any life can be improved, I hope.

The other way that negative thoughts can affect us is physically. If we are not mentally strong enough to project everything outwards, maybe our ego isn't strong enough and we are defeatist in our selves, then the physical body begins to mirror the damage in our energy field and chakras. Something goes wrong in our bodies; and what do we do, we hop off to the doctor for some pills and comfort. Nothing wrong with that, and the pills fix the physical problem, but they don't and won't fix the problems in our H.E.F.'s. Then we feel sorry for ourselves and add those miserable thoughts to the damage that hasn't been fixed yet! Go figure; have you realised the need to tame your thoughts yet?

Subtle energy always tries to work with us, and remember, the physical plane is just that, if you need to be stopped in your tracks and shown the error of your thinking ways, wouldn't you rather it was a stubbed toe than any of the above? I'm sure that you would, at least you would know that you know how things work right?

Why do we persist with the thoughts that bring us the negative feelings and events? In energy terms the brain is the vehicle of the ego and it does not want to relinquish command, remember the ego sees the word 'relinquish' as 'death of ego.' So logical, but emotionally-laced negative thinking is the remit of the ego and the brain is its external projection device.

The ego has a superb trick to stop you getting to the bottom of all this. I call it the mental/emotional flip-flop. First the ego convinces us that the only way we can deal with the nasty world is to build all these thought produced mental constructs that will defend us. Except it's forgotten to mention that those thoughts will be back soon, with some mates, and they will want to know where the party is at, and it's your energy that they'll be feasting on. Cunning plan part two; having convinced you to project the thoughts and reap the damage, ego then gets you to bristle at the results. 'Told you so' it whispers like Grima Wormtongue from Lord of the Rings, 'we are here to help you, they are not...' So instead of seeing the folly and heading toward a new way of thinking it's back to the familiar patterns, and so the circle world is perpetuated and continues.

We exist and work in a predominantly low-frequency environment that is very easy to mirror, we can easily slip down into the frequency of 'tick-tock' and everyday thinking. So it is easy for the mind to mirror its surroundings, and as we so often see disaster, death and destruction in the media, how do we know that we have to protect ourselves even against exposure to this level of negativity?

Big towns and cities are not conducive to deep meditations or clear energy-spaces, unless you go to a temple or a church, or a healing centre. That isn't to say that if you live in these areas that you can't raise your frequencies, you can, but you have to start somewhere. In this case I would buy some energy and thought space; get hold of a CD of good vibes, or a meditation session, and do them. Get an MP3 of inspirational speakers like Wayne Dyer or Stuey Wilde or whoever you are drawn to, and put them on your mobiles or i-thingies, protect your thoughts with higher energy and use them, don't just stack the boxes on the shelves next to the books that you are going to read one day!

Or you get thee to the countryside, or a nunnery, or even a park with decent spaces. Shift your body into a space that will give your mind the metaphoric room to breathe. Be aware of your thoughts, there are no correct justifications, all that mental skulduggery is your ego trying to keep you damaging yourself and in the same place, but leeching away your powerful subtle energies.

Let's try something that I was taught a long time ago that always works for me. This exercise is to show you how thoughts play a big part in the way that you feel, emotionally and physically.

For this session you will need some gentle music in the background, something pleasant, but not so strong that it takes your attention away from what we are doing here. Perhaps you could have some incense or a candle, whatever it takes for you to relax physically. If you could manage it a really good place to do this would be in the bath, but if you can't don't worry it will still work effectively.

Sit in a comfortable chair, or lie on a settee or bed and make sure that you are comfortable. Close your eyes and relax. Breathe deeply and slowly, allowing your chest to rise and fall gently.

Concentrate on a point just behind your eyes and try to imagine a small blue flame, like a pilot light in a boiler. Don't screw your eyes up and furrow your brow, no need to try too hard. When you have done this, step back from your thoughts and watch what happens.

I bet that some random itches and twitches will start, that you suddenly have to move? Still the body and ignore the itches, remember that you are stepping back from these thoughts. Keep the flame going nicely and then watch for images forming, don't react to them whatever they are. I bet that there are now some memory thoughts intruding by now, forcing you to look at the day's problems?

Don't react to them, step back from them, and just enjoy the little blue flame. You only need to do this for about ten minutes, and then let it go out and gently open your eyes.

What you did was to reclaim your thought space for yourself. By stepping back and not reacting to whatever was presented you refused to implement the ego's agenda of worry and strife. Each time you do this you remove a connection to a thought that restricts you from manifesting the life you desire, you reclaim a part of you that wrong-thinking has taken. If you can find time to do this every day, or when you feel stressed by emotionally negative thoughts, then you will be sending a powerful signal to higher energy that you are willing to work and to do what is necessary to reconnect. How can it not respond?

Thinking is a powerful manifestation tool and it is ours to use as and when we please. I hope that you fully realise that the circle world of the ego does not want you to think for yourself, it does not want you to be free; it does not want you to be using the power of thought for your life, it wants you in emotional bondage. I do not desire that for you, I desire freedom for you and your thoughts; I desire that you be able to concentrate on you.

Chapter Four

Where Are You Now?

The title of this chapter doesn't refer to your geographical location, no, what it means is where are your feelings now? OK you are reading this book so your energy will have calmed down somewhat, but you will still be feeling or thinking something. The H.E.F. is a dynamic system that ideally needs energy flowing through it constantly to do its job, there is no way, on this Earth anyway, that it can be doing nothing. There can be no way that there is no interaction between the H.E.F. and the world around us, even a damaged field is trying to repair itself and re-connect to source.

We are what we feel, or more accurately, we are what we think after we have emotionally interpreted the energy that we perceive around us. It's harder to understand and interpret the world positively when we have blocks in our chakras and H.E.F.'s.

Blocked or 'stuck' energy will keep the area of our lives that it corresponds to at a low frequency, and this leads to confused thoughts and angry feelings. Say we had a blocked or damaged Identity sector, with a negative charge of emotional energy sloshing about there. It would be hard to feel good about ourselves, and we would bristle easily and be very aware and self-conscious of that area of our physical bodies, we would also be likely to misinterpret any good intentions from others. We would feel frustration at the lack of good things happening to us, and we'd interpret the stuck feeling as a loss of some kind.

Until that area is cleared then this block remains and will negatively colour our lives and our thoughts and choices. It also affects how we approach things; a naturally positive person will keep trying in vain to get clear of frustrating blocks that repeatedly appear in their lives, sapping their self-confidence and optimism. A sceptical person will see their doubtful outlook and cynical thoughts verified again and again, justifying their pessimistic stance. You could put them together and each would argue through the same blocked energy but from their own perspectives;

"Told you so," barked Cynical Sid, "I just knew that this was my luck, what do you say to that, then?" Hopeful Harry winces but puts on a winning smile, and says,

"Look Sid, it says in my new book that you have to keep trying, until you win, and we have to win!" They both stare wanly down at the pink ticket, on which the register girl has kindly written a big black 'L',

"Same numbers next week Sid? You've got to be in it to win it!" Sid growls as he digs deep into his pockets,

"Another quid wasted, fourteen million to one are the odds!"

I can't say myself who will win it, but I know that their stuck energy can only bring them back to the ticket machine and this same conversation again and again. There are many souls on Earth stuck in similar loops of 'going nowhere energy' like the hapless Sid and Harry, and they have no idea that they are even stuck, they think that this is what life is actually about, unconsciously living their lives by the tenet,

'Life's a crock and then you croak!'

Stuck in a form of energy stasis that consists of continuous doing with little or no outer or inner improvements, they can see nothing other than the ends of their noses.

Our souls are impoverished whilst our closets are full of clothes and our bellies are full of food and other stimulants, which hold us in a perpetual need for more of the same. We lock ourselves into a kind of future mystical yearning for fame and fortune and the winner of next year's Kentucky Derby. We want a 'now' that is fabulous and amazing and smashing at the level that Enid Blyton's Famous Five used to experience it, yes, that good.

We are sure of this because the media always tell us that 'it's' all 'out-there' for us, all we have to do is go and get it. But where from, it may as well be on Mars! I want somebody to tell me where 'out-there' is, answers on the back of a postcard please. If there was one phrase that succinctly sums up the circle world of the ego, then that is it.

"What's the truth then Steve?" I hear you plaintively cry, pleading again I see? Well the answer is pleading obvious, even to me;

There is no out-there! There is only in-here, in you, in me, in all of us.

There's where the problem lies, we are so used to projecting all our thoughts and hopes and dreams and desires 'out' into the 'there' that we don't spend any precious time 'in-here' inside ourselves. We are glued to the window looking out to sea and waiting for our boats to come in, and waiting we will continue be! What was it Diana Ross said?

"..And I'm still waiting...Oh-woa-woa-woa, I'm just a fool..."

And she was right, we're all still waiting, waiting for the boats to come back, trouble is we've forgotten that we never told them to go out in the first place. So we're waiting for a random boat to come back to us, and it doesn't know where we are anyway, the odds are getting longer; still it's nice by the window, watching the boats going out and coming in again, for someone else.

We need it to be you that it is happening for, we need it to be you manifesting your hopes and dreams, we need to bring you back from out-there, and we need to re-educate you into the soul-groovyness of the in-here, we need to bring to you your true peace, grace and destiny. Your immortal soul will thank you for it and your dainty little pinkies will look even nicer in your Jimmy Choo's shoes, honest, would I lie to you? Where do we start then?

We know that stuck energy and blocked chakras need to be re-connected, and we're sort of half-willing to have a go; but never forget that pesky ego, once you start having positive life-changing thoughts, you can be sure that it will be on your case and pronto like! It will cod us that this is just another fad, another self-help book like all the others hidden away on the top shelf; and anyway they'd all just laugh at you down at the pub, or the health club. What you need, says ego, is more retail therapy, that new card has got a few hundred credit left, and after all, what's it there for? You need another ten CD's, a new suit, a top or a skirt, more shoes, a holiday, a car, another massage at Madame Wai's, it goes on and on. Do all this material stuff, but whatever you do, don't believe all this spiritual rubbish.

All of the above are nice in their place, apart from Madame Wai's, but the less said about that the better, but none of them, except this book, will do anything to plug up the holes in your H.E.F.'s that your vital life force energy is leaking out through. They promise that they will, and so does your ego, but they don't, and when they don't you have to go and buy some more, always searching for that elusive 'out-there' answer.

The only way that we can begin to fix our H.E.F's is to take everything one little step at a time. We need to imagine our feelings and emotions as a party size bag of fun-sized chocolate creamy bars, and not buy a half pound slab of whopper choc, hoping that we can nibble our way slowly through it Hamster fashion. We can see the little bars and consume them slowly, but at no time will it seem like a gargantuan task that we can never achieve. When we have completed each bite-size segment we can replace the empty wrapper and 'see' what we have accomplished in front of us. The half pound block will always daunt us and we will feel sickened at the amount of 'stuff' that we have to process.

We all have layer upon layer of wrong-thought, of misguided choices and actions, of erroneous emotions, and violent or angry, or cruel reactions to slowly remove from our energy fields. Nobody can deal with the enormity of that task instantly and completely, even admitting to the need for it is a decision of mighty proportions for a little human being. But we do have the capacity to change and reverse all the negative stuff, we all do, all of us, we just have to approach it now, and be in-here and not out-there.

We must begin by deciding that we will look intently and honestly at our fears, because we have to start somewhere, and they are a good place to find the root of our energy problems. Or at least where they are being perpetuated still. As we are only beginning to look at the way that our own thought projections create our life experiences, it's important that we avoid any recriminations about ourselves; after all we are the only people that can forgive ourselves.

How many times have you heard someone utter this immortal line:

"...and I'll never forgive myself!"

We know that they don't really mean it and that it is actually them asking for forgiveness from whomsoever else is involved, but, and it's a big but, the energy of this statement is powerfully negative. Its root is in fear, and fear is a powerful energy that affects us physically as well as energetically. What this person is saying to source energy and their higher-selves is that they are beyond forgiveness. That they cannot and will not accept the idea that they can be redeemed, that this wrong cannot be righted, how else can energy respond to that other than to confirm the command?

We need to look at powerfully negative statements like this, and there are many, and realise that their utterance is like a hoodoo and a voodoo on us. They may appease the ego's need for our supplication for our wrongs, or our humiliation in public in front of the wronged, but it doesn't stop there. In energy terms you may as well have 'slap my chops' tattooed on your forehead, or 'idiot, please manipulate.' These phrases aren't just social 'feel betters'; they are very powerful affirmations that carry executive command power. Am I making this clear enough?

As I have explained previously, even when we are working positively and ardently to fix our H.E.F.'s we face many challenges that we have to break down into manageable chunks. So how difficult do you want to make it for yourself? You already have a damaged and probably only partially- connected H.E.F. with some blocked chakras and stuck energy, and the various problems that come from that, and now you want to add the negative idea that you can't be forgiven, and you think love and positive energy is going to come from that?

'Worries' are the same, except they work the other way round. Worry is a thought process that comes from the fear that things aren't working right, that the universe isn't right, that the people that are the focus of the 'worry' cannot cope with their lives, or the outcome of their choices. If we are actively 'worrying' about someone we are creating problems for them, not helping them. We are projecting the fear that the 'future' that the person is heading for will not work out right. When we verbalise it we are doubling its negative power by directly spouting the fear into their energy fields. The irony of this is that we express worry to show that we care about somebody, that we love them! Hoo-ha, not quite what happens, but very typical of the circle-world.

Even if we really love the person that we are 'worrying' about it is still energy from fear and ego, and it does not help the person in any way at all, in fact the opposite occurs. Worry is the ego's way of saying;

'listen to me, I'm very important, I'm higher than you, and I know, because I am projecting negatively into your future, that you cannot change your life for the better, in fact, it will get worse, because I am worried, and that's why I am worried, because I know best.'

If that's not bad enough then listen to this part; when the worrier projects at the worry-target, that energy becomes stuck within their own H.E.F. too, and unless it is specifically cleared it hangs around their earlobes, doing what? You guessed it, creating more worries for people and things to be worried about. It is quite simply the easiest way to feel sorry for yourself and others in a way that is perfectly acceptable in the circle world, and it is also the easiest way to muck things up quickly and consistently.

If somebody says to me that they are worried about me I simply say, "Why bother, I'm not." I distance myself immediately from any emotional 'concern' they may have, and any reaction to the 'lack of concern' that I have. You should learn to do the same; I know it's difficult if it's your Mum or Great-Aunt Agatha, or your partner even. But they are doing you no favours by projecting fear at you. I do understand that they would be 'offended' if you said anything, or 'upset' that you didn't appear to care, and If you don't want a 'scene' then the best thing to do is smile sweetly and mentally affirm that you are not worried and have no need for those projections, but mean it, really mean it.

Now you can see how fear and projection works; if you don't want the projection, the 'worry', and you state that kindly and positively, then you get the sucker punch, the double-whammy of the 'I'm so offended' energy projection straight back into your chops. As I told you a few paragraphs ago, if you can't forgive yourself then others will see that tattooed on your forehead, and they will act on it, and worry about you. Like all energy exchanges it takes two to Tango, there isn't a one-way street in the human energy field, or there shouldn't be, and worry and other fears can only create problems for us all now, and in the future.

So if the above problems are affecting us now, and yet the energy came from a previous time, then we must have an emotional point of creation, or thought, that we are coming from now. If our desires aren't actually coming to us now then what are we doing that isn't bringing them? There must be an energy difference between what we think should be in our lives and what is actually in our lives. There is, and I call it 'the distance between', Stuart Wilde calls it 'variance' and covers it a lot in his fantastic books, so it must be important.

Most of the time, and especially in people with disconnected H.E.F's, what we think we desire is far, far away from us. And I would go as far as to say that what we think we want now is confused by and more importantly caused by the disconnected H.E.F., this is what causes us to keep getting what we don't really want?

Eh? I know, it's confusing, but so much of the circle world of the ego is about face like this. What I mean is this; when the energy field is disconnected from source and healing energy, all our desires come from the thoughts that we create whilst observing the TV, the media, and magazines and shopping centres. In short, consumer goods and articles of high-value that only people of high individual worth can buy, and better or prettier, more talented people that we believe we can never be.

So whatever we desire it has a pound sign before it, or it is a physical desire fulfilment and these are all external things that require certain conditions to be met, whether that be more money, better looking, fitter body, better job, more prestige...the list goes on and ever on. None of them are for, nor do they fulfil, any real purpose. The only benefit we receive from them is that others will perceive us as 'greater', 'better' or 'wealthier'. You can also be sure that none of them would make us finally happy, after a while of having them we would desire more or better, or a newer model, and that goes for people too. That doesn't make material things, by nature, bad, or wrong. Far from it, they are fun and frolicsome, if they have purpose in your life.

For us to achieve meaningful desires we have to start from the point that is the beginning of creation; why do we need them in our lives? That is the emotional point of creation; do we want stuff to make us feel better about our awful and horrible lives, or, do we want the stuff because we know that we love it, and can share it, and can feel good in the world by owning it? There is a huge difference between the two, and that is the difference between. The gap in creation is between what we think should be here and what we actually attract from our position of neediness and 'don't-we-deserve-it-after-all-we've-taken-from-this-nasty-old-world' ness.

It's as though we have built an energy version of a red and white striped barber's pole that stands between our chests and our desires. In our need we push forward and strive to get to the desire, which can only have one outcome, it pushes the desire that exact distance away from us. This happens every time we try it, and when we sit down to gently weep (with our guitars?) the pole stays right there, and when we awaken the next morning with renewed intention and a battle plan, the pole is still there.

We have to stop striving and pushing, to stop begging and pleading, we have to reduce the size of our barber's poles. Men; please don't go round telling people that you have to reduce the size of your barber's pole to get what you want. Honestly, it's not worth the looks, and people would worry.

When our manifestations do not match our desires then this is a sure sign that there has to be stuck energy in our H.E.F.'s, and we are more likely to be acting to the script of an energy pattern made up from earlier disappointments. What is interesting here is how these negative emotional energy patterns keep tricking us to repeat the same behaviour again and again, producing the results that we do not want or even like. Why haven't we recognised them yet, why don't we 'see' what is going on in our lives? Is it that we are so used to these things happening and the resulting disappointments, that we just accept them as the 'norm' that life is for us?

It just so happens that I can help you here; I can point you to the hidden patterns that trip us up time after time, we have a word for them, moods.

"I'm in a mood, leave me alone," "she's moody, best we leave her alone,"

Any of these phrases familiar- sounding? Apart from full-on rage, there is nothing that looks or feels as negative as the H.E.F. of somebody in a 'mood'. We describe these people as 'under a cloud' or as 'thinking black thoughts,' how apt these descriptions are, and another example of common phrases describing what the energy actually looks like.

One of the more difficult aspects of learning about our H.E.F.'s is that we have to, at some point, take back control, or in other words, accept more responsibility for our feelings, thoughts and thought projections. There is nowhere that is further away from that acceptance, in energy terms, than being in a mood. There is no mental and emotional state that totally gives away control of how we think and feel than the 'mood'. We have a great word in English for the total 'giving away' of any responsibility for anything; it is called 'abrogation.' Quite simply, 'mood' equals 'abrogation'.

Being in a 'mood' is a churlish visual statement that we etch on our faces and project through our folded arms and crossed legs. We are denying any further interaction with positive or healing energy as we declare to the world our disappointment with its choices for us. We are giving signal notice that our ego has duly noted the terrible transgressions perpetuated upon us by the evil world around us, and we are showing this with our petulant display of inner 'harrumphing' that could match any 'terrible-two's' display from a toddler.

The most amazing thing about these negative emotional states is that the mooded-one is perfectly aware of the destructive nature of their state, and the realisation of this just throws them deeper into the morass of self-justification than they were before. Whatever breakdowns of communication or destruction of relationships that occur as a result of 'moods' are not seen as the fault of the moody type, they are just the other people being awkward and hurting 'them' more, even more justification for the mood. The other amazing thing; well, when the mooded-one is given what they want for the mood to stop, and everyone to breathe a sigh of relief, they have to be coaxed into behaving nicely again, and the others have to tread on eggshells around the subject for evermore.

Now that's what I call a winning control strategy! If only the outcome was positive. Unfortunately that is not the case. In this particular control drama an energy imbalance has been created, a negative surge of emotional energy has 'stolen' the outcome from the people that give in to the mood. The mooded-one feels justified in their actions because of the desired results, but it has left them with an energy deficit, and because the 'mood' was negative, then the energy that fills their H.E.F. is entirely negative.

Let me explain; moods are made up of low frequency mental/emotional energy that we project outwards from us. They begin because we note that something doesn't seem to be going our way. The ego acts in its usual selfish and circle-world manner and comes up with a defensive attack strategy 'before' we get 'hurt' or, not get what we actually wanted. The ego does not want to ask or negotiate for its desires; it expects that they should come as planned, in the right amount and at the right time.

Ego 'sees' the contradiction that the world places upon it, and acting negatively, it must save face, it must put the discourteous and disrespectful ones in their place before any damage to its prestige is done. This action is the circle world at its lowest and best frequency, this is where it lives. To be 'offended' we have to have a previous position where we considered ourselves superior, whether we will acknowledge it or not. Better that we do deny it for the ego, because then it can run its 'hurt innocent' pattern, where the 'bewildered good person' just has to react to the onslaught upon its righteousness from the unworthy, 'your honour, I give you Hollywood!' case proven, no contest.

Moods have their own self-protection system that in itself proves the low and icky frequency of their energy. If you were in a mood and I came along with my chirpy, cheeky-chappy good-natured positive-ness, how would you react? C'mon, be honest? Look you're amongst friends here, you can tell the truth. Right, you'd get worse wouldn't you, and you'd resist the onset of positive, loving energy, because your H.E.F. is entirely shut-off to the higher and the healing energies. If you are determined to act, think and feel ugly thoughts, then a beautiful energy coming along and whispering gently about your greatness and soul-majesty, would only get your 'backup' more, wouldn't it?

Therein lies the problem, and again we are back to 'the distance between' phenomenon. We can't snap out of the anger and nastiness because we are too far away from the healing force of the universe, and we have shut up shop. We are locked into the frustration of the mood and its yucky thoughts, and we will soon begin to feel it physically, in the form of headaches and belly aches, and many other aches too.

Our friend and guide in these situations is the step back from the feelings into observation. The only way we can begin to come back to healing from this place of isolation is to stop reacting to the negative feelings before they overwhelm us. 'The Doors' put it beautifully in their song 'People are strange.' These words describe the positive energy isolation that a 'mood' creates;

"People are strange when you're a stranger, faces look ugly when you're alone, women seem wicked when you're unwanted, streets are uneven when you are down."

I don't know where you are in your feelings now; if moods do dominate at times, then we need to look at a strategy of avoiding their onset. I realise that when there are blocks in our H.E.F.'s then it's much harder to see those blocks as the source, but we've also discussed that whether we transmit energy positively or negatively is our choice. Hmmm....a conundrum, a loop that holds us in this negative state called 'mood', we've been here before haven't we?

The beginning of any journey starts with the first step, at least that's what some obscure Chinese philosopher said about a lot of centuries ago. Great! That's a help thanks, I'll remember that! Get me! Witness the outpouring of sarcasm, what has happened to my spiritual outlook? Why can't I say, "Thank you Confucius old chum, sage advice, and I will take that much vaunted first step right now." I can't do it from a mood because from my position of isolation I look at spiritual things with suspicion; well they obviously don't work do they? I wouldn't be miserable and in a mood if they did, would I? look at all the books I have bought, look at all the courses I have done, load of old hokum, I'm still getting depressed, I'm still in these moods, but what can I do about it?

OK, when we are this far in as I was in the above example, then damage control is necessary. We really need to get some stuff that will make us feel better; whether that be pizza, grape-flavoured falling-down juice, or a hot bath with steaming herbs and spices, or all of the above, and slice of cake, chocolate cake. But no television, and only classical music or a relaxation tape. Also, try to be on your own, and then you can choose how you spend the time you have to fix yourself. I also wouldn't recommend any activities based around physical excitement at a time like this, it might seem like the right kind of emotional release, but it is actually a confusing addition to the morass of feelings. Only when we have reeled our H.E.F.'s projections in a suitable amount and we feel calmer is it safe to go to bed, to sleep.

The most important factor in understanding and fixing energy problems is getting to know the emotional point at which we start getting into them, and why they keep happening. Whilst we are working hard at trying to comprehend all this we also need to keep a strong sense of perspective. We mustn't move into the negative recriminations that lay all of the blame at our doors.

Until we are in total control of our fixed and healed H.E.F.'s we will be spending a lot of time moving through a lot of energy systems and energy fields and projections that aren't our own. As if dealing with their many random thought projections wasn't enough, now we have to cope with and understand energy imprints.

Energy Imprints are what others project out into the world from the isolation of their moods and negative thoughts. We could imagine an imprint as a snapshot of all our feelings, good and bad, beamed out from a broken energy field from a hurting mind. Whilst you are healing yourself and mending your broken wings, you stand next to someone who doesn't feel as good as you, and 'bam' they project onto you their fears and negative energy. In a second you go from trying to comprehend your feelings to fumbling in your pocket for a ticket you know that is there, it was a minute ago. Immediately that negative imprint takes you back to 'people are strange...'

Where is our emotional point now? We are now splurged with another's yucky icky wickedness. What can we do? We are back to the disaster plan, and whilst that might be nice, again, it's getting us nowhere fast. This then becomes a loop of getting a little better then getting splurged, and then we hit the bath. Three steps forward and two steps back, then two steps forward and three steps back, and repeat. This scenario is quite normal for a lot of people on this planet, living their lives with little or no connection to higher or healing energy in a perpetual state of feeling drained physically and emotionally.

We have to come back to the two basic tenets of energy work and this little book: They are: we have to start somewhere, that is 'here' and 'now', and we have to take things one at a time in 'bite-size' chunks. That's all well and good, but how do the two tenets apply here, what can we do as a coping strategy that will also move us on? Good question and one that I am going to answer now.

What we have to do is look at how we start each and every day, and I'm not talking about the eager expectations or miserable mumblings of the night before. No, I actually mean the way we think and feel as we wake up and begin the process of facing the day and the world again. We know now that thoughts transmit both negatively and positively, but it is much harder to accept that ability to choose in the morning.

What we are running through our minds on awakening is running to the bathroom and then coffee and breakfast, and whatever other tasks that face us. What time do we have to meditate, to contemplate our navels, when other people are crying for their cornflakes? I understand this and nowhere else in our days do we greet our basic humanity than in the morning, but we know that we have to start somewhere, so let's take a little look at what might be happening in our H.E.F.'s every morning.

If we start the day with our connections to higher and Earth energy disconnected, or only partially connected, then that morning consists of the blocks and constructs of all of our previous days that have led us to where we are now. So we start the day with a reaction as all those unprocessed and ungrounded feelings flood back one by one.

Imagine a computer re-booting after it has been shut down because it is infected with a virus. Has that virus disappeared because the computer has been shut down for twelve hours? Do we expect that when we restart it the virus will somehow be gone? Nope, as soon as we fire it up and the power floods through its circuits, then that virus is there and active and affecting the operation of the computer, whatever we try and do with it, until the virus is removed.

We are the same, except our computer viruses are the blocked and damaged chakras; we go to sleep expecting to feel better because we had a hopeful outlook, but we awake and as we interface with the world again and begin to fully inhabit our physical bodies, then our H.E.F.'s attempt to reboot and reconnect to the better energies. When they can't do that then all they can do is to re-run the energy patterns that we have in our H.E.F.'s, whether they are ours or someone else's, that is all our higher-selves have to work with, until we change that.

Simple hope cannot create the life we desire to have, nor can it reconnect our H.E.F.'s. It is very hard for the universe and higher energy to hear your call when you aren't connected. Instead of a one-to-one mobile phone connection that is intimate, caring and always responding to your desires and interested in what you are doing, by hoping and wishing you are trying to shout across a busy mainline railway station platform that you don't have the right ticket for the freedom train. No wonder that the guy in the ticket office is looking bewildered. But what he will do is point at the stairs that cross the platforms to where he is, but you have to recognise that and trot over to him. Then he'll tell you that the train has left, but hey, you've got a dialogue going.

Walk with me across the gantries to the other side of the railway station where the Pullman lounge is. C'mon; it's morning, we're out of the bathroom and down the stairs heading for the cornflakes and toast. Our heads are full of the day ahead and what we are going to do, and the tasks we need to fulfil to get our families going too. What can we do to help the all too familiar scenario before the negative constructs start to fade our positive energy and attract to us the very events that we don't want?

Take a few minutes for yourself after you have done the necessary tasks, go and sit somewhere quiet, or at least less noisy. Let your brain rest and become quiet as you sit still, or lie, breathing gently as you let your whole body relax. Don't think anything, and just observe any thoughts that flibbert into your mind space, don't react to them, just observe.

Accept that your life up until now has been a construct of former disappointments that you have reacted to. Forgive yourself (very important) and forgive god, and forgive the world. Even if you haven't got the conviction of these thoughts yet, still do it.

Be grateful for everything, even the bad stuff, it brought you here didn't it? Speak some words of gratitude in your mind, however opposite you feel, speak them. Something like, 'Thank you for everything in my life, every moment, every second, every breath, thank you.'

Allow all the things you desire into your life, give them some space in your energy field. Say to the universe, again even if you don't yet believe it still do this, 'I allow all my desires into my life now, and thank you for –whatever it is you desire most- as I receive it into my life.'

This will take no more than five minutes, but they will be a very important five minutes, indeed they are the building blocks that will lead you to the full re-creation of your H.E.F.'s and enjoying your lives as you desire them. There will be more energy exercises and ways to reconnect as we go further into the book, but for now this one is excellent, and remember, it's a bite-sized chunk of spiritual choc that you can munch on here and now.

If during the day you find yourself lost again, or harassed by another's bullying manner or energy imprints, then just repeat the gratitude affirmation, and allow peace, grace and love into your lives. You can do this, you will do this, and I wish that excellent and joyful reconnection for you all.

Chapter Five

"I react therefore I am."

So far I have been discussing with you how higher energy and healing energy connect with our physical selves through our H.E.F.'s, and what can and does happen when that connection breaks down. In the rest of the book I'm going to be talking about how we 'react' to the energy that encounter during our day-to-day lives, and how that creates energy patterns or 'states' that we then repeat and suffer from in our inner lives.

Every person that we meet and every situation that we come across can only reflect to us how we feel at that point, this is the emotional 'point of creation' that we met in chapter four. Sometimes a person that we meet is so powerfully positive that they can blast through our resistance, but even then we might choose to react negatively tightening up our protective shell that keeps others out, and us in. Not everything or everyone is negative though, and often the universe tries to bring us to the metaphorical crossroads and gives us choices. This is the root of the saying that goes

'Fear not to entertain strangers, for you may be entertaining angels.'

Of course we also have to entertain discretion, and this is why intuition only becomes powerful and correct in its intimations when we have started on the road to fixing our H.E.F.'s. We can find the crossroads and the angels in human form, but we have to be past the point where all we can see or perceive is the darkness in other people. They are also processing their shadows and doing the best they can do considering their lack of connection, whatever they look like. When I first started on this path I had a really difficult time with the darkness in people, especially when I encountered it in someone that I cared about or loved, close friends too. I will admit that I reacted to it, and became deeply upset that everybody was so dark. I didn't come out of this self-imposed depression until I realised that the mirror of energy was showing me that we all have our inner shadows, and we are all here to integrate and process them that I could stop reacting emotionally.

The circle world that we live in is a world of reacting to outer events that have been brought about by others reactions. We are trained from a very early age to react to what we see and hear, and we incorporate it into our daily speech and it colours everything we do. Climatic conditions are especially sent to have a go at us, "its awful isn't it, this rain?" "What's happened to summer?" "It's too hot; there'll be a drought next." Whatever the weather does we aren't happy, and react to it, the fact that is simply 'the weather' doesn't matter to the reactive self. Everything is polarised into black and white, everything is for or against us, she loves me – she loves me not.

This cannot help us in our plan to reconnect with our H.E.F.'s, because the energy that we project now is what creates our future now's, and what we are experiencing now, is a result of previous thought and feeling projections. The reactive circle world keeps us reacting and disapproving and feeling bad about things until finally our limited capacity for negativity tips out and floods into our lives. Our ability to feel positively and see brightly diminishes exponentially, and our choices begin to fail us and we judge others indeterminately. Suddenly two slices of big fat cake seem like a very good idea, and now we understand what happy hour is really about.

If these reactions continue for long enough then we can begin to make poorer choices that can literally change the course of our lives, for the worse. It is much harder to see that it's all for our own good when we are looking in fear at a mugger, or the car behind us slams into us. But these options are there in the circle world, and it has many others too offer on its smorgasbord of horror events, just read a newspaper or watch the news, but only a little bit at a time, don't get sucked in too far.

What do we call all this; fate, destiny, bad or good luck, a deity's whim at our behaviour, good fortune, bad fortune? Actually it doesn't matter what we call them, because we've ordered them with our projections, and they are faithfully on their way to us. That is the point of the circle world, it applies meaningless labels to things that behaving in a reactive manner will bring anyway. That is what the saying 'be careful what you wish for, because you just might get it' is really telling us; whatever we wish for, it is our reactive behaviour and projections that bring us our day-to-day stuff.

Unfortunately this also means that ignorance is most definitely not bliss. Or rather, the lack of knowledge of what we have created for ourselves is blissful because the stuff hasn't hit the fan, yet. Despite our best 'intentions', as long as we include ourselves in the reactive way of life of the circle world then we can only expect more of the same, and hopefully it won't get worse, but it probably will, it always does, doesn't it?

Did you spot what I did with that last sentence? I let it slip into the reactive way. There's no way that I would want to think or feel like that, but if I had spent a whole working day dealing with low frequency energy, then that would probably represent a thought choice that I might make. It is really easy to fall into because it is all around us.

Poor energy choices are often the reason for the phenomenon of good people becoming victims that the media is so fond of throwing at us. It may seem awful that lovely Mrs Miggins at Number forty- six was mugged and left bruised, when she had never hurt a soul in her life, but what we cannot know are Mrs Miggins thoughts and feelings for the previous sixty years or so.

It seems harsh, but that is the way of the reactive circle world, she could have been projecting the fear of being alone and even of being mugged for many years. Energy works, both positively and negatively, all the time, it doesn't give you time off for good behaviour, nor does it forget when you've had a bad day. I wouldn't want this to happen to Mrs Miggins or anybody else, but until she changes her thoughts and feelings, then that is what she is creating.

The hardest part of leaving the circle world of reactivity is the realisation that we ourselves are responsible for our energy, and that we ourselves will have to clear up the mess we have made, and, worst of all, that its' nobody else's fault! But of course taking that responsibility has to be done in a non-reactive way, not "Oh well, if I have to," or, "What a palaver, where's all this come from then, whatever next?"

There is no doubt that it is difficult to see the wood for the trees, and that the fog of obfuscation that the ego generates is difficult to see through. So, what I'm going to do in the rest of this chapter is to describe some of the most common negative energy patterns that the circle world projects at us, ones that we all have faithfully mirrored, until that is, we know better, which is here and now.

The 'Stingray' Complex.

You can hear that manic bongo theme music belting out from Gerry Anderson's 1960's kids puppet show, and in the background Commander Shore intones the legendary phrases,

"Stand by for action, this is battle stations!" and,

"Anything can happen in the next half hour!"

This is disaster management at its human finest, we slam into the day, caffeine and ego-fuelled, undaunted by yesterday's failures and determined that today we will win, we will overcome, again.

This person has decided that the world needs fixing and they are up for the job. They are a pro-active type that is always reacting on the inside, and they have very active egos. They are always sorting other people out and coming to their rescue, and sage advice is never far away. Trouble is that they never sort out their own problems, kidding themselves that their constant badgering interaction with others somehow exempts them from having to deal with their own inner turmoil.

The other problem is that their help is purely external and empirical, in terms of H.E.F.'s they are actually draining energy from others. What they can never tell the people that are close to them is that they are coming from a complete lack of self-worth, but that is disguised by the ego with blustering false pride. Of course the energy mirror is working full on here, they really should listen to their own advice, and indeed that advice is coming to them from their own higher-selves in the vain hope that they will listen.

Another side effect of this approach is that their emotional energy is building up in the background, but they are neither accessing it nor even countenancing their feelings. Emotional energy cannot just dissipate, it has to and will channel, and if the native is not directing it then it implodes physically. If we consider that the H.E.F. equivalent of this is an overactive third eye chakra and a blocked heart chakra it doesn't take much imagination to see what problems might occur.

How many times have you heard about someone having a heart attack or similar, and then be told that the person was an avid runner, never smoked or drank or did drugs? That is the power of subtle energy in our lives, it needs to be approached and dealt with, or that energy will implode in our H.E.F.'s causing major problems.

The fix for this person would be the opposite of what they would think. They really need to stop, right now. No more meetings, no more committees, or tap-dancing or Mexican Iguana juggling sessions. I think that if I said the word 'meditate' they would run, or more probably buy a CD, then transfer it to an MP3, then transfer it to their I-thingy, then buy special water-proof earphones, then listen to it whilst they were jogging or in the gym, or at Salsa class…you get the picture. If you know someone like this tell them to slow down, or say, "You know when you told me I had to slow down last week, why don't you try it?"

The 'Chicken Licken' complex.

'The Sky's falling in; the sky's falling in…' We all know this famous line from the old children's fable, and we are sure to be able to recognise the hysteria of Chicken Licken in the daily newspapers and on TV. This reaction is their stock in-trade, and they rely on our reactions being like Chicken Licken to create and support their business. But as always in the circle world of the ego there is more to this than meets the eye, which is even truer in the world of subtle energy. Just who is being the Foxy Loxy here, and how does this apply to the people we know?

This is a very common energy pattern amongst people; you might even say that this is the basic way that reactive people with disconnected H.E.F.'s behave. The media are the Foxy Loxy in this they just pretend to be Chicken Licken. Governments use the same pattern; constantly wringing their hands and telling us that there is nothing that they can do. They know what they are doing; they want everyone to do a Chicken Licken so that they can offer us a 'solution' that always costs us in some form or another. This is pure, unadulterated Foxy Loxy, and we the people are all Chicken Lickens in their book.

When this pattern starts to dig in it can really get hold of people and it creates tremendous problems and damage in their lives, and also creates a base feeling of fear that is very hard to shake off. This fear is insidious and it pervades all our thoughts, making us feel trapped and lacking. This creates a powerful inner urge to project outwards, we need to justify how bad we feel, and so we need to feel that others are suffering just the same.

Out goes Chicken Licken and gathers information through chit-chat, gossip, text messages, phone calls, newspapers, and internet websites. They need assurance that they are not alone and insurance so that the 'inevitable' disasters that 'will' befall will be paid for. They become a roiling inner mass of contradictions and judgements, fears and anger, jealousy and envy. They become controlled by Foxy Loxy, identifying themselves and their moral base by their purchases and their power to purchase. The 'must-have' drive becomes unbearable and yesterdays baubles and bangles become useless and trash when this weeks batch of 'new and improved' bangles come out. Like Pavlov's dog these lost boys and girls are led by the nose to the nearest shopping centre or website.

This **is** the circle world, this **is** the way that the Foxy Loxy controllers want us to be, and don't expect Cocky Locky to run off for the Kings Guard dogs either, there is no rescue party, it ain't going to happen, and anyway as long as you can buy more things then ego is happy. If you can't buy more things then ego will turn their heads to credit cards and loans and re-mortgages, and when this goes belly-up, theft and extortion. It's a slipperyslope that many are on, but in truth they don't care, they are in deluded consumer heaven, they don't even know, or care, that this is an energy pattern. "Anyway what's that fool Oakes talking about, I've just got the latest catalogue, and this seasons shiny things are in, where's that credit card."

When people are grabbed by this pattern, then the basic fear and ego -controlled pride energy makes it very hard for them to see that they have any problem, they just need more stuff, and then everything will be OK! The basic rule, that you have to start somewhere, applies here more than ever. The first thing these people have to do is to come out of denial, but it will be a hard job dragging them out of 'Howdy-doodle' magazine and out of the shopping centre.

If you know anybody that is seized by this pattern and you feel that there may be a shadow of a doubt in them that their world might be unreal, then in the words of the great Wayne Dyer, they need to 'Simplify, simplify!' De-clutter and not buy anything for at least twenty four hours, forty-eight if they can manage it. They need to get to a position where they can slow down the roundabout, after all their frantic pushing, only then will they be able to get off. The hardest thing for somebody coming out of the Chicken Licken complex is that they need to learn to be alone, they have to stop craving and arranging the company of others. They have to come to a point where they begin to feel OK with themselves, and then, and only then, can they begin to reclaim their inner space and rebuild their H.E.F.'s.

The 'Hollywood and TV' Trap.

The worldwide film and TV industries are immense and they have two very influential and powerful products; they are the films and programmes themselves and the stars, the so-called celebrities. Combined they have a far greater power than most people give them credit for, in fact I would go as far as to say that most people are influenced one way or another by these two.

The films are lavish affairs that cost many millions of pounds to make, and a lot of time, they are stories presented visually, with the added power of having our complete concentration. We are affected by the 'hype' around the latest blockbuster and we queue around the block to pay to watch them. Because the people that make them are themselves famous and glamorous, we view them with avid glee, hoping to find existential answers beaming out at us from the screen. Or they provide a more visceral experience with horrific and graphic violence, and the pornographic ones supply something else entirely.

What they actually do is engage our entire range of emotions and feelings; we fully give of ourselves as we sit wilfully imprisoned in our seats, watching and waiting for the message from our screens. To see the full effect of the film experience and how it affects our H.E.F.'s, stand ninety degrees to the side of somebody who is watching a film on TV, dim the lights, and watch the light rays batter into their H.E.F. On top of that is the sound and the emotional and mental experience of the action, it is total energy immersion, and we are at the mercy of those who have made it.

What few realise is that those rays have power, and they carry the same effect of what they portray, of course it isn't the same as actually witnessing what is portrayed, but over time that effect builds up as a toxic energy within our energy fields. Then we begin to become inured to the effects, it is easier to watch graphic horror and violence, and we can mentally step backwards saying to ourselves that it's "only a film." Worse than that, for our watching pleasure that is, we get used to the same outcomes, and can often guess most plots and plot devices, the audience becomes cleverer.

What do the film makers do? They have to keep us glued to the screens, whether we are at the drive-in or at home, they must keep us interested. What they have done, and still do, is to change the outcome of a plot that we know, girl doesn't get boy, girl gets mangled in crossing- road- for -boy horror. More than that though, they have had to make the main characters more dysfunctional, more 'realistic' to the viewer's eyes.

More and more the main characters reflect lives similar to our own, and guess what? The bad guys are getting badder, as the need for more violence and graphic nastiness increases, and I believe that this is having an effect on our energy. I call it the Hollywood trick, and what it does is quite simple, though often hidden in complex plots. What it does is to leave us powerless, and I don't mean powerless to leave our seats, no, I mean powerless to change, powerless to get ahead, powerless to have a good life that we affect with our own positive thoughts and feelings.

As people watch the effect of horror after horror unfold on the witless hero, and their efforts become less effective and more is taken away from them, and more damage occurs in their lives, they are damaged more than words can say. But they soldier on until they succumb to whatever nameless horror claims them. The bottom line on this contract is that we are powerless against, the muggers, thieves, gangsters, corrupt police, rapists, murderers, serial killers, aliens...it goes on. What we need are superheroes; Batman and Spiderman, kids that can do magic, bigger guns, faster bullets, spaceships, the common cold... Because we couldn't possibly do it for ourselves could we?

Yes I know that we are supposed to be only suspending our disbelief, but we are so used to immersing ourselves in this emotional experience that I do not accept that most do just that. Instead they watch the screen and the stars, as they act and cavort in a world that seems so similar to our own, surely they will find the answer, and they give their whole hearts and energy to the film or TV programme.

Then as we confront problems in our own lives the echo of these experiences replays in our heads; insidiously they whisper like Grima Wormtongue from *Lord of the Rings*, "there's nothing you can do, this is what it is, and there are no rescuers for you!" Then instead of life being an experience that we create ,it becomes a 'harsh reality', we read and hear phrases like 'in the real world', or 'in an ideal world yes', we see that nothing is working, and that our frenzied efforts bring us back to the same point. The Hollywood trick is effective in our energy fields, so what do we do, we watch another film, or a film that evokes in us the feelings that we are experiencing, and what happens? Our energy plummets down and we feel the sadness and the poignancy that we are watching for the umpteenth time *magnify* our negative emotions, and we believe that this emotional state is how we really feel, how we are, and that we are powerless to change.

It is a very powerful effect, and it works for violence and horror too, and all the other genres. OK I'm not saying never watch a film again, that would be silly, but I would say give them up for a while. Try it and you will see how hard it actually is. Sitting in a quiet room with a darkened screen in front of you is a sobering exercise if it's for the first time. Even if you just have one day a week where you watch nothing, you will be giving yourself emotional space to be free, for a while. Another method may be to try to watch films that are non-violent, see how hard that is, but there are more spiritual alternatives these days, and I hope that there will be more in future.

The 'Cult' of Celebrity and TV 'Reality' shows.

Today this is a rapidly growing industry that shows no signs of receding in popularity. In fact I'd say that its increase is exponential and almost guaranteed to succeed. There are magazines that are just about 'celebrities', people that are famous for being famous, and increasingly, famous because they have been on a reality TV show. Websites all over the world update themselves almost by the minute as the latest hot poop comes in on the 'now' celebrity, or the former golden one whose star is not just fading, but plummeting into forced re-entry and the certain burnout. TV programmes tell us what the magazines and websites tell us every day, about people whose contribution to the world I simply their increasingly botox-filled expressionless foreheads and bright-shiny bleached smiles.

Why are they so popular, what is it about them that makes so many people follow their every move? It's quite simple really, it could be us up there, it could be us on that football field earning amazing amounts every week and fighting off the attentions of glamorous others as we cruise into swanky restaurants, reservation not required. It could be us being followed by cameras, being interviewed for our precious opinions, being invited to the Bafta's because we are 'it' that week. It could be us walking into the best clothes shops and walking out with a flunky carrying the bags of clothes that we weren't required to pay for. It's a heady mix, and the con is that it could be every one of us, it could be. So what is the energy in this, what relationship does it have to our H.E.F.'s and how could this affect us?

As human beings we become greater and more by energy exchanges and by energy increases; we improve ourselves, our lives and our relationship with the universe through the correct actions of our H.E.F.'s. As our moods wane and we connect to higher and healing energy, there will follow improvements in the 'whom' that we are. From this good things will come into our lives, the level of which we decide. This is all with the caveat that we have healed our H.E.F.'s and re-connected to source.

Not many celebrities have done the above, in fact most of them haven't; you can tell that by the antics that they indulge in daily. It is obvious that they believe in their own importance, to the point that airing their dirty laundry is their M.O. Oscar Wilde (allegedly) once said that 'the only thing worse than being talked about, is not being talked about', and there is nowhere that this applies more than in the world of celebrity.

So when ordinary Joe or plain Jane from hick town becomes propelled into the spotlight they are obviously delighted and lap up the limelight. But what they don't realise is that the position is not a steady job, along with all the wealth and possessions they are given a long pole and they are pointed to a nearby tightrope. They are primed and expected to fall, to fail miserably in the public eye, and we watch eagerly, nay baying like hounds at the scent of Foxy Loxy. Each of their precious 'things' that they adore so much, has an energy, a monetary cost, that they didn't have. So they don't truly accept that they deserve them. Guilt and fear about losing what they have been given drives them to search and clamour for more, in the hope that their outrageous behaviour somehow justifies what they have, that it demonstrates to their adoring fans that they do deserve it all.

Then they do believe it, and after a while the adoration and attention become second nature, then they believe that they should have more lovers, more cars, more houses, and more free stuff. They become petulant and childish as they clamour for more, until the almost inevitable fall, when the same people that gave them the stuff take it away with equal pleasure. They never realised that the energy wasn't theirs, and as mentioned before, their own energy fields do not have the energy capacity to accept wealth and possessions responsibly, so the energy takes itself back. Because it was never a debit, it was always a credit. It's as if the controllers of celebrity gave the hapless celeb a credit card with no credit limit and a personal pin number, in the meantime nothing was mentioned as they racked up a huge energy and monetary debt, then as the ivory tower tumbles they re-appear and say to the celebrity and say "How would sir/madam like to pay the bill? Option one; a soul-searing public humiliation, and then a slink back to ordinariness, Option two; a soul-searing public humiliation followed by extensive examination of your sad demise as you cling to fame and fortune." We've all seen it happen, probably more than a few times too, but how does this affect us, after all we aren't the celeb in distress are we?

Well in a certain way we are, and I want to talk to you about that now. When we are observing all this happening to the celebrity or the downed politician we think that we are impartial observers. Well actually, that is the way that we need to be, but it is rarely what we do. What we do is we hiss and cluck and 'tut-tut', "always said she was a wrong 'un", "had to happen really didn't it, with her background!" What are we doing, we're judging them, applying our vigorous moral standards (that we always adhere to!) to their sad lives and calamitous choices. When we judge somebody else it isn't just our brains that are activated, our energy and our H.E.F.'s are too. In fact our chakras go into overdrive, attempting to connect with the remote figure on the TV, or maybe it's just a picture in a newspaper. OK this connection is not the same as actually being with the person, but it is still a judgement placed and that is what does the damage to us.

If we are moving forward with our H.E.F.'s and starting to release blocks and clear our energy paths then we need to be impartial observers and not be in judgment of anybody. As soon as we do this then we are mirroring our judgement on the celebrity, and that energy has to come back to us. It will come back even more quickly with a remote figure because as soon as it realises that it has no other H.E.F. to poison and infect it comes straight home to Momma, and that's us. It has the effect of holding us in that negative thought pattern and keeping us rooted right where we are. Better we acknowledge the trap that they have fallen into and resolve not to do the same thing ourselves by judging them.

Exactly the same methodology is involved in the new wave of 'reality' TV shows, where we are invited into the lives and the very homes of the great and famous for live and impromptu displays of their dysfunction. Or, we watch contrived shows where disparate people are thrust together in a hostile or claustrophobic environment and guess what is going to happen? Quite what people expect other than the dire results that they see I don't know? It brings the judgemental voyeur out in all of us, and encourages us to slate characters for their behaviour. There are programmes after the main events that focus on the audience reaction and talk about what has gone on as though it is a valid event, that the things that have occurred have any actual importance.

It's a very clever trick, and we are mainly hook, line and sinkered into reacting good and proper, even to the point of developing dislikes of people that we don't even know. This is so far from walking a mile in another man's moccasins that we may as well be judge and jury ourselves! Kangaroo courts erupt all over the land as the participants are judged entirely on what is shown to the willing audience. It really is not good for us to be indulging in this kind of behaviour, but the 'reality' ticket just pulls us in there, and suckered we are.

As with the Hollywood trick, I am not saying that we shouldn't watch films or read magazines and watch TV shows about celebrity. No, what I am saying is that until we have re-activated and re-connected our H.E.F.'s then we should cut back on our intake and diet from judgements or emotional trips, thus we allow our energy to fully re-connect and normalise. We have to learn to discern, to choose wisely and watch and read only those things that support our positive emotional and energy development, and in that way we move forward at no energy cost to ourselves.

Chapter Six

"Three steps forward, two steps back."

In previous chapters we have learned a lot about how we interface with our immortal soul through our H.E.F.'s, and how the ego ruled circle world creates blocks within it that change how we experience our lives. I have frequently mentioned that the circle world does not teach us about our H.E.F.'s and how that knowledge has remained mostly hidden. I'm sure that by now you will have decided that reactivating your H.E.F. would be a very good thing to do, and that energy work is your way forward. You have the powerful and positive intention to move forward. Fantastic, what could possibly go wrong now?

Well, you have to remember that you are coming from the circle world, and what has been mainly in charge during your stay? Yep, you've got it, your ego, which, let's face it is perfectly happy with the arrangements in the circle world, and doesn't want anything to change. It's a peculiarity about ego in the circle world that it doesn't mind if things are awful in our lives, in fact it thrives on all the trouble, convincing us that this is all normal. You could say that your ego isn't listening to all this new age mumbo-jumbo. It's probably got its fingers in ears and is placing on the big pink and furry ear muffs as we speak.

You are probably wondering why I am rabbiting on about this ego thing; after all the whole thing is just a decision isn't it? All we are doing here is deciding to do something about it; it can't be any harder than that, can it? Well, sorry to be the party-pooper here but there are many ways that the ego can trick us back into the circle world. You could say that is has a number of excellent weapons in its arsenal, and it wants us to be stuck in the same-old same-old, yet again. Do you think that after all these years of trying to run your life that ego hasn't noticed you striding past the Ben and Jerry's in the supermarket, that it hasn't clocked you trying not to react to others' annoying behaviour? Think again, it has, and it knows you are reading this book, and is planning the best way for you to backslide even now.

We need to start by getting to a place from where we can make positive steps and move forward, but to do this we have to understand the ways that ego and the lower-self can trick us into negative thinking again. We need to grasp how ego and the effects of the external circle world subconsciously push us into the same self-defeating behaviours that have traditionally caught us. We have to take into account the many previous times that we have run these negative energy constructs before, and how they often 'appeared' to be useful in the past years. It is going to take both effort and time to shift them out of your energy, but I highly recommend that you attempt it.

All this time our ego will be throwing bogus statements into the mix, all designed to confuse and dismay. Things like "Life's not fair," and "What have I done to deserve all this?" It wants us to feel self-righteous and special but somehow overlooked by the good stuff, punished by a cruel god and a meany-pants universe. This is one of the ego's favourite cons that can easily throw us into a loop of self-pity and back to the litre-size pots of Ben and Jerry's! But the Universe has no emotional reaction to the state of our lives; it thinks that we want what we've got, why, because we asked for it. Source energy cannot feel sorry for you or empathise with your plight, so kicking and screaming about the unfairness of it all is fine with your mother or your best buddies, but it won't cut the mustard with the universe.

I know, I know, this journey out of the circle world and into the higher energy can be very difficult and frustrating at times, and there will be occasions that you will question the worth of it all, even to the point of thinking, why bother? That is exactly what our egos and the circle world wants us to think, and where they both need us to be, in a position that is static and full of negative emotion. But I am here to tell you that this journey is very worthwhile, and unlike the mythical Jason we may not get a golden fleece at the end of it, but we will regain positive control of our feelings and thoughts, and that has to be worth it, and believe me, your immortal soul will thank you for the spring cleaning and makeover.

OK then, guys and gals, lets take a look at some of the methods that ego uses to trick us, it's a tricky little tyke and that's for sure, and it will never miss a prank to play on you, or a mental loop that will throw you into the thinking heebie-jeebies.

First and foremost our egos will want us to abreact to this book and the information that I am imparting in your general direction. It will try and convince us that all this energy stuff is beyond us, that it's alright for him to go on about it, after all he's done, anyway he doesn't have the problems that I have, he doesn't feel my pain, does he? He couldn't use all that stuff in my life, and I bet that he doesn't do it all himself anyway? How could we possibly get time to meditate with the demanding and noisy kids, a screaming husband to feed, and then there's work too! Or; all the above and a harassed housewife to placate instead of a husband and somehow juggle all this, without thinking negatively, boxes of chocolates only work so many times you know?

You can see what I mean, can't you? The ego has years of practise at working on us, it knows all of out weak points and needs, and desires, and requirements, but it is not necessarily helping us to get them. No, it's just constantly pointing out that we haven't got them yet, and what can this silly book do, and what planet is this guy from anyways? There it goes again; having a good old go at us as we head for the chocolate solace department, or the wheat and fruit based fally-down water. I know that we all have boats that need floating from time to time, but we also have to remember that to float the biggest Ocean liner we only need to add water, and that even the biggest boats are not unsinkable.

Well if you've got this far without a raging ego, or even, as is more likely, with a raging ego, then you deserve congratulations and a hearty, if imaginary, clap on the back. There you go, consider yourselves beamed at and heartily back-clapped.

As we contemplate the re-activating and re-connecting of our H.E.F.'s we have to remember that the ego can only see its death, its certain demise if you carry on with all this stuff. It is staring at not being the big cheese in your mind anymore, and you can be sure that it will be looking in its 'bumper book of smoke and mirrors' to try and save itself. Ego won't take all this well or sitting down, even now it will be going into hyper-galactic overdrive as it comes up with carefully reasoned schemes to keep you exactly where you are right now. Here follows then some of ego's main schemes and ways of tricking us, some of the smoke and mirrors that have so far managed to keep us up to our necks in trouble and Black Forest Gateaux.

The Habitual Reflex.

There is only one thing that the circle world of the ego fears and that is the individual, the activated human spirit inside the fit and healthy human body, the person with the personal power to choose their own lives, the soul that brings down heaven on earth. The whole essence of the circle world is to keep us disconnected from source energy and healing spirit, to keep us thinking and reacting to the many troubles and tribulations that it faithfully supplies every day.

The circle world really doesn't actually want us to know that we are contributing to all these negative events with our thoughts. Does that sound odd to you? Why would it 'protect' us from something that would throw us into even worse abreactions and fear, wouldn't that further its aims to keep us in the dark and feed us doo-doo? Well actually, no, it wouldn't, and the circle world controllers know this. Why so, you cry? It's because that very abreaction at thinking that our thoughts are part of the problem, whilst causing initial distress and guilt, would be the first step in our release from the circle world, and the controllers know this. They really do not want you upset in a way that would de-stabilise the carefully plotted and planned circle agenda; they do not want you on the path to healing at all.

So then, how does the circle world of the ego manage to keep this information from us so effectively? One of its most effective methods, and this one works for a whole lot of people is what I call the 'habitual reflex', or as the French say "Comme d'habitude", we do what we have been shown to do, by the example of our parents and those around us, we do what we always have done. If nothing changes in our lives then we accept that and do not look to change anything, why should we? After all, doesn't the popular saying go "if it ain't broke don't fix it,"?

This may work in automotive terms, but it isn't the answer in soul communication and regeneration terms. If there is no change, no search for deeper meaning beyond 'what's the news today' then our life force becomes static and stagnates. Without a reaching for higher connection and healing then we can only fall further back into the doldrums and humdrum of the circle world. Everything around us can only become more boring and repetitive, and the corollary of this is...? You guessed it; off we go in search of stimulation, however we can get it, and whatever makes our cookie crumble. We will have it, because we have to fill the void of energy created by our habitual lives; whether we fill our boots with credit cards, with narcosis, or alcohol fog, or even food feasting, or all of the above.

That isn't the end of the influence of the habitual reflex though, oh no, the circle world isn't finished yet. What happens next then? Well, whatever we choose from the above becomes habitual! We get **used** to it; we increase the doses because we are bored with the circle world, but the cure itself is **of** the circle world, so however much we add to ourselves, we still come back to where we started, full circle.

Maybe we become more adventurous and seek another off the list, it doesn't matter because sooner or later we will become bored and jaded with that. Here is the habitual reflex in action. Now I'm not saying that all of us are going to crash and burn with this, no way, some do of course, and we all know examples of that. What mainly happens is that we become jaded and disappointed with life. The future that was so bright that we bought the shades becomes a fight and a struggle for more salary, more money, more everything, all in the hope that the 'more' or 'better' will feel differently, and then so will we, we hope.

When we become entrenched in the habitual reflex in the circle world, then our H.E.F.'s can only slow down and this will always affect our actual lives. Two particular energy areas that are badly affected by this energy pattern are the heart and solar plexus chakras. They slow and eventually stagnate as they fill with emotional pain and unresolved issues that are still causing us pain, we begin to lose sight of who we are in this world. Each day can become a dull repetition of the previous one with no light at the end of the tunnel being only the start of our problems, we may actually find that no one has told us where the light switch for the tunnel is, and even if we find it, someone has forgotten to change the bulb.

It is sad when people get this far into the habitual reflex, because they lose contact with love and caring, first for themselves and then for all other people around them. Whatever method they have chosen to escape the dullness that they perceive their life is, the method will, after time, and much concerted application, eventually envelop them and reclaim them, this energy pattern is very powerful and insidious.

The lyrical French language has another word to describe what the habitual reflex creates in our everyday existence; it is called **'denouement'** and it describes the final revelation or act in a play, where all is revealed and we know what is going on. So, in the worst expression of the habitual reflex our days become a succession of denouements, or efforts to rationalise or understand what has happened to us so that we can get on with the next day of circle world sameness. But how can we understand events that seem to randomly happen? We can't, so instead we react to those events emotionally and resolve them incorrectly, with whatever poison we have chosen to apply for solace from the very real emotional pain of the circle world. Remember, it is real to us because it is negative emotional energy stuck in our H.E.F.'s. Remember the Blondie song 'Denis, Denis'? Well I'm going to paraphrase it terribly here (but actually quite appropriately, Denis being a patron saint of France!) and give us a saying to break out of this. Instead of happily singing "Oh Denis oobido, I'm in love with you..." I'm changing it too, "Oh <insert your name here> oobido, don't do the denou!" Don't do the denouement, this is the trick of the habitual reflex, the day is ours to change, it is always here and now, we are always renewing and receiving, if only we will allow it and accept it, if only we choose to change and clear our H.E.F.'s of this painful blocked energy, and to move into a better day.

'Common Sense' hidden pessimism virus.

No matter how many times we are told to 'listen to common sense', 'to toe the line', to give up on 'pipe dreams', that a bird in the hand is worth two in the bush, or any other balloon busters, we always hanker for more. The immortal spirit in all of us reaches far beyond its grasp hoping for more than this, more than the local shopping street, more than the TV. We are willing to read books, poetry, contemplate art, listen to music, drink in a beautiful landscape, and enjoy an uplifting film. There are many ways that show the expressive creativity of human beings.

Yet often even the artists that create such haunting expressions of their creativity are often themselves haunted and chased by inner demons. Why aren't they healed by this expression, why aren't we in turn healed by that expression? They grasp a sliver of moonlit stardust and show us what they have found, and we respond to that with a knowing that can sometimes be startling. Yet there must be a reason (says common sense) why these people are not healed, or seem to be incapable of healing themselves, that is, of course, assuming that they identified the need for that healing themselves.

There is a reason and I call it 'hidden pessimism', it lurks just underneath the empirical linchpin of the circle world, common sense. This concept is drilled into us from the word 'go', we are told that we should have our feet on the ground that we shouldn't dream, that we should work hard, that we are here to work, and it's unfair. We are infused with a deep-down core disbelief that any of this energy stuff is true, or, horror of horrors, it might actually work. The circle world starts us off with this plugged in and hard-wired into our minds.

It is a virus that has infected many, many of us, and it says that we can only rely on the empirical and scientifically repeatable things. We can only believe what we see with our own eyes, anything else just isn't true. It has created a division that has on one side the fundamental religious types, and on the other the intellectual nihilism lobby, neither meeting, nor neither allowing the other credence. There is a tenet in military tactics that states that' to conquer an enemy first you must divide them', and nowhere will you find it being expedited so expertly as here and now in the circle world where we live.

This is where the hidden pessimism hides, in our divided minds, and it is the direct result of our being hammered with the common sense argument. Instead of our character being allowed to develop and flower, thus allowing any latent abilities or talents to express themselves naturally, we are told what to learn, what to think, we are indoctrinated with others agenda. At first the soul revolts, when we are children we will struggle to express ourselves, arguing and railing at parents that are telling 'us' what to do. It doesn't take long for the imprinting of the common sense to start to remove our soul-connections sliding us back into the circle world.

This will continue until we heal our H.E.F.'s and reconnect to the source energy and the healing energy, or, if we don't do that, then this will continue. The soul will make attempt after attempt to get us to look at our spiritual and energetic selves with more open eyes and an open heart too, yet each time we reach out, the pessimism virus tells us that it's all just hocus-pocus, if it was true it would be scientifically observable and repeatable, would it not?

So our natural self-expression is beached in an overactive and yet still divided mind, separated further by the day, from a soul that is crying out for reconnection and healing. The restive mind then projects negatively into everything it meets, expecting the worse, and not being surprised when it happens, as it will. Oh how we wring our hands and there is much gnashing of teeth, our egos rail at us for our foolish quests for a better life. What use, it asks us, is this energy work? Can it pay the rent, can it stitch a wound, build an ocean liner? So we listen, we go to work, and we behave ourselves (mainly); why then, do we keep finding ourselves at the 'mind, body and spirit' section of our local bookshop?

Two steps forward and three steps back, disheartened we face another day and another solace session at the end of it, and yet still we try, we push on, we go back to the bookshop again. We search for the goodness inside us whilst only spotting and highlighting the bad, we try to share our love and only notice the faults of others. This is the hidden pessimism at work, the false and implanted belief that at some point, when we don't know, everything will go wrong for us, like it always does and did. But hey, common sense says that we just carry on, get on with it, accept our lot, and be a good little drone. I know that it's a grim view, but this is how powerful the virus of hidden pessimism is, and it is lurking underneath all the 'common-sense' tenets of the circle world, and the ego is its main proponent.

If this seems all too familiar to you, or it applies to somebody you love and care about, then you know what I am going to say don't you? You've got it! You have to start somewhere, and that where is here and now.

This is one of the deepest programming patterns of the circle world and it is difficult, but not impossible, to shake off. We have to start from a little new thought and then we have to build on that. Shakespeare left us a little clue in his play Hamlet, who famously says,

"There are more things in heaven and earth than are dreamt of in your philosophy, Horatio..."

We would do well to listen to Hamlet, and to realise that to create a new energy start for ourselves that we need to do a little mental spring-cleaning. We have to start with a releasing thought, and then ignore the inevitable screeches of the ego and its 'common sense.' That thought needs to be a personal affirmation to ourselves, one that is easy to do and yet still challenges the hidden pessimism of common sense. Here's on that has always worked for me, I first read it in Stuart Wilde's 'Affirmations', and it helped me a lot at a time when I was beset on all sides by the denizens of the circle world.

"I am Eternal, Immortal, universal and infinite."

Try that for a while, and see how many times your ego tries to force you to forget it! Another that works well to unravel hidden pessimism is;

"I am fit, healthy and super-wealthy!"

Make your own up, have a go, it won't hurt, and anything that heads you back on the path to reclaiming your soul-self has to be good, capice?

The High Energy 'return drop.'

There is no doubt that beginning the path toward reconnection and proper soul activation is a powerful and proactive decision to make. It usually comes after a lot of thought and consideration, and not some little desperation at the state of our lives. Ever onwards we forge, and we pledge that nothing can stop us as we sally forth into the great unknown.

Friends and family are constantly amazed at our staying power as we embrace change and let go of many of our self destructive ways. We get through the initial stages of self-doubt and self-recriminations, and we push through reticence and disbelief into a new area of life that contrasts greatly with what we have known before. We feel great with our new sensations and the subtle feelings of energy, we are connected and intuition runs high as we allow all our faculties through.

It's a powerful and great place to be and we are exultant and proud of our achievements, we know that the manifesting world is our oyster and that now, finally, we can achieve what we truly desire from life.

After the struggle for attainment of high energy, reconnection and healing, we truly feel that this is a battle we have won, and to the victor goes the spoils of war. Hang on a minute though, and 'whoa there Bald Eagle' for good measure! Battle, Victory; aren't these the terms that the circle world loves so much, aren't these part of the lexicon of the ego? Where have they come from and how have they sneaked back in? I thought that the bouncers had thrown them out; they haven't got tickets for the high-energy ball, have they?

It's the siren call of the circle world; you didn't think it would let you go that easily did you? It triggers your pride in your achievements, but because this is ego we are talking about, healthy pride turns into decidedly unhealthy hubris. It's like those adverts for high cost vanity products that tell you to buy it, because you deserve it, or you're worth it. What they can actually do and what they actually offer pales into insignificance next to the hubris of being 'worth it'. I'm not saying that you shouldn't buy these things or have them, no, what matters is how you are triggered into buying them with the leading phrases above.

So what is the 'return drop'? Well it's the effect that causes us to go back to old habits after we have cleared our energy fields, and it is greatly magnified because we believe that we are beyond these effects. That is how the ego traps us and the circle world welcomes us back with open arms; it's like when you leave a troublesome service provider, you forget all the bad times after a few months, and sure enough, six months later you get a pretty card with a message that goes like this.

"We're sorry that you left, we're missing you, was it really that bad? Here are some free gifts for when you return." The nerve of some energy providers! But do we bin the card; do we tear it up and swear to all that can hear that we are never going back there? No, we look at what the free gifts are whilst generalising as we rationalise, 'well, they weren't that bad really, were they?'

The sirens are calling and they are calling us on to the rocks of despair. Let's say that one of our problems was that we drank too much wine, we weren't alcoholics, but our intake was definitely a bit too much. Now that we are energy workers we are past that now, and we don't need to return to it. But the ego hasn't finished yet; we receive an invite to a wedding where we know that our friends will be living it up, and lapping it up too. At first we think that we should avoid it, we don't want to slip into old habits after all this hard work. That is the right instinct, and we should follow it, but do we? Then a random thought slips in as if from nowhere; 'why not go, it'll be fun, and we deserve some fun don't we. It will be a great opportunity to show how stiff our resolve is.'

Isn't that a good idea, we erroneously think, and off we go to the wedding decked out in all our glad rags and feeling very proud of our achievements to date. Half an hour in and an old friend walks over with a glass of wine...you're ahead of me aren't you? What do we say when the friend says 'go on, it's only one glass, how can one glass hurt you?' One glass of strangely delicious wine later and you are eyeing up the second, then the third, and on it goes.

It's not drinking the wine that's wrong, and it's not that the wine is intrinsically evil, it isn't, (and we can all enjoy alcohol sensibly) it's the quality of the energy it represents to us that causes the damage. The massive drop in energy that this particular intoxication will cause comes because of hubris. We are going against the sage energy advice of our newly connected emotional advice system, we are doing this because 'we' deserve it, because 'we' have worked hard to get this far, why shouldn't we have some fun? But we aren't far enough away from the ego effects of the habits that we have left behind; their siren call is still strong in our hearts, and we mistakenly believe that we 'deserve' them.

Why is this wrong then, why don't we deserve good things? This is why the return drop is so hard to understand at first, it just seems unfair that we can't have what we desire, especially after all our hard work. There lies the flaw in this logic though, energy is not saying that to live a high energy life you can never drink wine or enjoy yourself, you can, but with one very important caveat.

*It has to be a conscious choice that you make, an energy decision that you are happy about, you have to **love** that glass of wine!*

All the ego-driven siren wails of 'why not', 'you deserve', 'you're worth it' et al, simply put you into a state of wanting to be rewarded, demanding to be fulfilled, especially after all your 'hard work' getting this far. They do not allow you to choose, they force the ego-riddled circle world back into your heart. They tell you that this new life has robbed you of your joy, that it cannot be any fun in this world if you can't drink with your friends. So you grab the opportunity and imbibe away, safe in the knowledge that you deserve it. But source energy knows that you chose the immediate fulfilment over conscious choosing, and sadly, it backs away, again.

In many ways it echoes the fall from grace; those that have higher knowledge choosing unwisely and reaping the whirlwind. Trouble being that because it drags us back into the circle world of the ego, it has to be active, it has to be justified, so it has to repeat and even increase the activity that caused the fall in the first place.

As with all energy work there is always an answer, there is always a way out, but we do have to choose it. The return drop isn't just limited to alcohol; it can be applied to any addictive substance or mental or emotional or physical activity. The answer is to be wary as we move out of the circle world and make every-thing we do a conscious choice, and if we really do want to go to the wedding and get giddy, then we have to choose to go, to say to ourselves that we know and understand that there will be negative effects but that we accept responsibility for them. This way we can avoid the return drop, we will still have an energy drop, but source energy will stay with us, just don't do it every day, that's all.

The World 'coming at you'.

As you leave behind the lower frequencies of your life so far, you will often find yourself at odds with the places and people that surrounded you. Family and friends will often resist you changing your life, finding rational and sensible reasons for you to stay exactly as you were thank you very much. It's not that they don't want you to have a better life, it's more that they can't see theirs getting better if you skedaddle.

As you begin to change for the better and your frequencies increase, people close to you will initially keep up with you and encourage you. But as you appear (to them) to be accelerating away they may begin to become a little sullen and resentful towards your 'new life'. Plus they will also expect you not to be able to keep up the pace (see 'hidden pessimism' section) and you will eventually give up the silliness and return to the fold.

As the person doing the painful and stressful changes you would have expected to be supported rather than hindered, it doesn't seem unreasonable does it? But others can't see that, unless of course they are on the path of fixing their H.E.F.'s and reconnecting to source and healing energy, and that isn't very often is it?

Indeed the world will seem to be 'coming at you', and you will feel isolated and alone. It is a grey area between the circle world and the world of high energy that we all have to cross, it is a true 'No-man's land' that is really only occupied by negative energy. That is why when you first become energy- aware; all you can perceive for a while is the negativity in people. I mentioned this earlier in the book.

I feel that there are lots of people in this world that are trapped in the grey area of negative energy, not part of the energy world, neither are they fully in the circle world. They hover around, sad and disenfranchised by a world that they feel has left them behind and doesn't care about them. Paul McCartney mentioned it in the Beatles song 'Eleanor Rigby' he wrote;

"All the lonely people, where do they all come from, all the lonely people, where do they all belong?"

There isn't a way to get from there to here without crossing the no-man's land, and we can't help but find and see the lonely people, in fact that is what we contact in everybody we meet when we are passing through here, the loneliness in everybody. Without wishing to dwell on this area, as human beings we are all born with a sad song somewhere in our hearts, I believe that it is a soul memory of the collective pain of humanity, and that we have to have it to be able to learn, understand and even function emotionally on the earth plane. It is the place that stops us from meltdown, which makes us keep trying to find answers, and why so many of us feel alone without anybody else around us.

We find it hard to stop people resenting and resisting what we are trying to do, and even though they do have soul recognition that they are being left behind; they just don't recognise it consciously. Your path to higher energy and a fixed and healed H.E.F. is ahead of you and around you at the same time; and you will advance as fast as you can evolve, and once you get into conscious choosing, then truly only you can stop you.

If a situation or a person cannot go with you on your energy path then you have to face that at the moment their evolution is not yours. You will have to let them go with love, and you will have to embrace the positive change that you have invoked. When you have healed your H.E.F. to the point that you are fully functioning and re-connected, then, and only then, you can go back to the old people and places and re-embrace them, because you will then be able to support the amount of love and energy that they need. Then you will have crossed the grey area and you can look back over the No-Man's land and smile at the reactive person you used to be.

When you get past the 'world coming at you' you will really have taken your life by the scruff of its neck and hauled it into a positive present. I'll finish this section of my book keeping the Beatle's theme and will say that to have come this far you really have taken a sad song and made it better!

In the second half of my book we will be taking all the knowledge that we have learned and applying it to 'real' life situations. I will end with some deeply spiritual words from John Lennon and Paul McCartney that really mean a lot to me, from the song 'Let it be.'

"**When the broken-hearted people in the world agree, there will be an answer, let it be,**
For though they may be parted, there is still a chance that they will see,
There will be an answer, let it be."

And remember, 'all you need is love,' sing it, sing it from your heart, 'all you need is love,' let it be.

Part Two

Energy in Action.

When we first boldly venture onto this path of being an energy worker in the Circle world, one of the more difficult aspects is our impatient search for immediate and visible results. The amazing revelations of our H.E.F.'s and also the heretofore hidden world of subtle energy and its manifestations often push us into a state of heightened expectation, and, for now, unrealistic goal setting. We are also confronted with the huge new idea that we are somehow responsible for how and what we feel and think.

Whilst at first this is a big scary idea, it can quickly turn into a feeling of the huge potential that our lives can hold. Immediately we leap into a furore of smiley feelings and inner declarations of intent; I can have this, I can have that, this is mine, they are mine too, it's all mine, I tell you! Yes, of course, with proper manifestation and the proper time taken to heal our H.E.F.'s it can be that way, but what we forget when we begin to accept our great potential, is that we have to get there from where we are here and now.

If the things or the conditions or the people that we desire aren't in our lives now, then there is an energy distance between us and them. But the conscious mind races ahead of where we are now, that's understandable and very human. This can create disappointment though when the desired effects fail to materialise immediately. How else can we see things at this stage in our developmen? We are conditioned by the circle world to its repeatable and visible system. For example; we strike a match, the flame ignites, the match burns out. Simple and repeatable, and mostly guaranteed, and happens instantaneously.

Subtle energy doesn't work like that though; it takes both time and effort to make it respond. But when we contemplate energy work it seems to allow all the desires and 'can't haves' back into our minds, and suddenly we are actively desiring them again; there's nothing intrinsically wrong with that, and let's face it, desires are the basis and the beginning of the path of manifesting our desires into our lives now.

What if I said to you that you can have everything that you desire, but it would take you say thirty years, what would you say?

"Forget it, I'm out of here, can't wait that long, what's the point of that?" OK, but what if you are, say, thirty now? Then, what you are now is the result of thirty years of **not** manifesting what you desire. You accepted that and carried on in hope and the desire that things would improve. What if accepting that it might take thirty more years to manifest is the very trigger that allows it to come now? It would be remiss of me though to suggest that just doing a rain dance and intoning 'supercalifrag-ilisticexpialidocious' ten times a day will have everything you desire manifesting in your back garden now, no, that really would be something quite atrocious. I'm not ruling out that potential possibility, but I wouldn't stand there holding your breath either.

What I am saying is that you will have to do some work on yourself, and that this process may take some time. How long I can't say, everybody is different; but I do know and can assure you that beginning to take responsibility for your thoughts and feelings and moving toward acceptance of the self, will start the process of fast tracking you towards your desires.

You have been ploughing through the seas of despair like a huge ocean liner with engines on full ahead, and suddenly you realise that you have been steaming in the wrong direction, you have to turn this ship around. It takes a lot of effort to stop and turn one of those ships, you have begun the effort by putting the engines into reverse, but it is still hard to turn those rudders as you heave on the wheel, on your own. But once you sincerely begin to take responsibility for your life as it is now, then powerful forces from source, that are unseen, will join you to aid you. Suddenly, instead of fighting the wheel –turn on your ship, you will have celestial tugboats pulling you around, and angelic bow-thrusters heaving you too, trust me, you will.

Having managed to get our noggins around the self-responsibility idea, the next struggle is wondering how all this talk of energy fits into the life that we have unwittingly participated in making for ourselves? How can we reconcile our day-to-day business that has been the same for as long as we can remember it, with this new world of subtle energy? Put simply, how the dickens does this fit into our lives?

Well, in the next few chapters I am going to take key areas of our lives and describe them in the way that they happen to us in the circle world, but from the actual point of view of the subtle energy from source. I will show you the ways that energy has always been working in our lives, and I will illustrate how it is us that have turned our backs on energy, and that it is not the other way around. This is the way that the circle world disguises subtle energy from us; it doesn't educate us at all in the ways of energy and the H.E.F. Instead it instils us with an intrinsic feeling of guilt; we feel that somehow we deserve the bad stuff, that we are being punished for doing the wrong things by a higher power that is jealous and vindictive. Worst of all though, it makes us feel as though there is nothing that we can do about it.

I will show you that it is very possible to effect positive changes in our lives, and more than that we can do it ourselves, without the aid of a safety net. We'll see that all we have to do to make a quantum shift in perspective is to listen to Richard O' Brien's Time Warp,

"It's just a jump to the left, and then a step to the riiiggghhht." We don't have to put our hands on your hips, but hey, you choose. Life isn't about leaping forward and forging on regardless, that's the circle world's idea. We don't have to give up all the good things to get into energy; we don't have to feel like Homer Simpson as he cries,

"Why do all the bad things taste so good?" We don't have to live in a cave dressed in sackcloth, painted blue, squatting on a wet rock under a drip for twenty years chanting 'ho-hum' for good measure.

What we do have to do is to stay where we are now and re-examine who we are and how we really think and feel, warts and all. We don't need to sell up and buy a quaint pottery shop when our inner-minx wants to be a belly-dancer, we shouldn't go against our dreams because they don't appear, right now, to be attainable, or they may be shattered and our feet will be covered in clay.

The point is that whatever and wherever you are in the circle world now may not be who you really are; it most probably is your best approximation of who you really are using what you had around you. Let's not disrespect ourselves here, clapped backs all round please, we've got this far, and that truly is superb. We have to give ourselves time to integrate the energy changes that will take place as we move into healing spiritually. Because I can assure you that the new you, the spiritually authentic you, may not be what you think it should be now. It could be something completely different, and there will be clues to our true identity inside us, in the desires we have previously felt impossible and the dreams that we have put on hold.

When I have shown you how subtle energy works in all areas of our lives then those clues as to who we are will begin to become more obvious. Once bare intentions have been stepped sideways out of the circle world's influence and into true knowing, then who you are can't stay the same, it will surge out from deep inside us where it has been waiting patiently.

Chapter One

"Food and drink - we eat what we are!"

I'm aware that the title of this chapter is the opposite way around from accepted thinking on the subject of food, but that statement is the energy truth of the matter. Many nutritional experts talk about calories and fat content as though that is all there is to it, they say what you put into your body has a corresponding food type and calorific value that then shows, or doesn't show on our bodies, as a result of exercise, or indeed, the lack of said. Or it could be that our metabolic rates are slower, thus we are fatter, or faster, thus we are thinner.

All of this is very hunky-dory, and easy to follow, so why oh why are we nations of dieters? Why do so many people turn to diets and fad foods and miraculous devices for help and why do so many people feel bad about themselves? Of course part of the problem is the way that we are sold the 'beautiful people' in magazines and on TV; how could we hope to compete with the Surgeon's knife and Botox syringes, and not forgetting the Art Editor's airbrush tool in Photoshop for those flawless orange faces and pencil- thin waists.

Many people are left feeling that they are 'wrong' and that they should somehow be like their perfect idols, they are forced into negative comparisons that leave them feeling ugly and lumpy, and because of this yet more will they will worship the Cocoa bean. So the energy answer to food is;

We are not what we put inside us; we are *why* we put that food inside us.

It's not the jam doughnut that's at fault, it has neither evil intent nor purpose, nor is it 'bad' by itself. No, the problem lies with how we feel when we secretly cram two of them in our mouths, at a time. What desperate need or negative feelings have caused us to do that? Are we responding to a denial of love, do we feel that something has been taken from us that we must replace with the jammy doughnut, or is the doughnut a reclaiming of personal power from the circle world?

We are the quality of energy that we feel about our lives, we aren't becoming fat ,we are pushing the world away from us, creating a physical barrier that pushes away the bringers of pain. It could even be a secret rage at the perfect people, an inner knowing that what they represent is false and is 'the Emperor's new clothes', that underneath the surgery they are just as lost as we are, and the super-whooshy creamy bar is a silent protest.

All of the above are conditions or states or negative feeling, of blocked and ungrounded energy, of lost vision and clouded logic, of a damaged H.E.F. We cannot forget that food also equates to survival and existential issues, and they are powerful motivators that require careful and firm handling. When they get out of hand because of energy field damage or dysfunction, then they will take control of our lives completely.

I also believe that we have a 'bogeyman' worry about the energy feelings we have about what we eat and take into our bodies, almost an instinctive knowing that things are wrong, and that they won't get any better by doing this, but still we do them. We 'defy' the bogeyman by feeding him, and in the process we program our bodies as to exactly what we want it to do with the taboo foods.

Our physical bodies are our most faithful companions in this physical plane; they carry us through the world day after day, giving and interpreting all the feelings and sensations that we enjoy, the smells, the tastes, sights and sounds, the ever faithful carrier and sensation centre. And more importantly they faith-fully interpret our energy messages about how we want the food that we eat to be processed. Minute by minute our emotions about and feelings for food are carefully interpreted by the physical body.

So I would view the body not as a temple, but as a gymnasium or an adventure playground through which we experience and interpret the world, they are where we work out and also, crucially, where we reap the energy feelings that we have sown into them. From chewing food to romping around, from walking in the snow to bungee jumping off the tallest bridge in New Zealand, they give far more than we ask of them, and some of us ask a lot. Yes it is true that source is always in charge of the basic running of our bodies, and we have little control over that, (and we should be very grateful that this enormous task is taken care of for us) but we are in charge of creating and managing the energy that we program the body with.

Our physical bodies will accurately apply the energy and thoughts that we have about the food that we eat to the food that we eat. They use these feelings to interpret how they deal with the food. This works in the same way as with our emotions, and all the negative thoughts that we have become the result of how our food is processed. As with everything else in the world of subtle energy, the resultant of what happens in our physical bodies is caused by the state our energy is in before we actually eat or drink.

Most problems with weight, lack of weight, or addictions, are caused by an energy lack; they can be fears, feelings of 'emptiness', energy blocks, or even an energy field damaged so badly that is has become a negative void itself. The food, drink, drug, is a vehicle that allows us to 'do' something whilst we experience these energy lacks in the vain hope that they will 'cure' or 'fix' the energy lack. We placate the pain inside us with the very thing that will increase the pain, and then on top of that, our bodies will process the stuff according to our pain and its intensity. As things appear to get worse, so will our bodies' decline, unfortunately this in harmony with our own wishes expressed through our troubled feelings and dysfunctional thoughts.

If the energy part of this energy equation wasn't true, then the chemical 'feel-good' factor of the food, or the 'happily-full' feeling would be good enough, and we wouldn't overdo it. I feel that this is also why so many people love and crave chocolate; I'm told that chocolate has about 550 flavinoids as compared to a carrot's seven. No contest, and such an intensity of sensation, both guarantees that chocolate sales will rarely drop and that our reverence to the blessed cocoa bean will only increase.

All of the negative feelings and thoughts about us and our relationships with food stem from our distance from source and higher-energy connections. They represent our unknowing search for that source energy without us even knowing what we are looking for or why. We are looking for subtle energy connections in physical sensations that they just can't provide, but because they are the strongest and most vital sensations that we can find easily, or not so easily in some cases, we repeat them again and again, hoping that the 'break on through to the other side' will come with the next fix, or jammy doughnut.

This is what the circle world is about, the illusion that the physical world has the answer to all things, that all we manufacture or create from the Earth's resources must be the highest of all cures. Why should we think any differently, after all it's not as if we have been educated into subtle energy is it? How can somebody that is in inner pain not interpret the circle world's sensations as the only answer? Unless an alternative is shown and highlighted, then its back to the Supermarkets and the Off-licence's for us, the conscious mind steering us back to that peak physical experience again and again.

Of course, with each experience the peaks slips further away and we are left with a lesser experience, so we must repeat it again but this time using more stuff in the hopeless search for more intensity, for more of that feeling of being in control of our lives, whatever the damage it may bring. We look for more reason to be here in these peak experiences, even if it kills us, or worse.

The circle world sees people with eating or intake problems as addicts, as people somehow emotionally crippled, as worthless, beyond saving. Well I'd agree with them having blocked and damaged H.E.F.'s, but I wouldn't accept any of the other descriptions. I see them as being waylaid by the circle world and its promise that the greatest sensations are in the physical world and that the brain and the body are in charge. These false assumptions create a sense of invincibility as the ego takes over the show and convinces these people that they are fully justified in whatever they do. No matter the tremendous cost in years of potential life lost and money, and possibly jobs, careers and families too.

They are far from their energy connections and each 'one-more' experience takes them further away from source. They are adventurers that are lost with no fix on their position, they don't know the way home, and they don't know that there is a home, namely subtle energy. These people have to reconnect, it probably isn't possible straight away for them to stop what they are doing, but their only recourse is to reconnect or a return to grace will not be possible.

I am trying not to be too specific about negative things in this section, but I do feel that this dysfunction requires a direct mention, namely smoking. Of course all smokers know that it is bad for them, and I won't lecture on the addictive qualities of Nicotine, instead let's look at the energy of smoking. Smokers know that it is bad and wrong, we all know that, but does it make a difference? No it doesn't, and why is that? Because the ego is fully in charge with smokers, and however they are picked on or marginalised they will continue to smoke.

In energy terms smoking denies life itself, it denies the quality of the breath that gives us life, it poisons the lungs and the blood-stream directly and also the energy of smoke creates clouds of mucus-like energy around us, and that's before the smell of it. So, it's a drug and it's bad for us, but you can buy it. So the actions of the circle-world in telling us that it's wrong and printing awful and dire warnings on the packets do what? They give smokers a nasty notoriety, which the ego loves; it's doing what it wants and beggars the rest of you, perfect ego scenario.

You can't 'give-up' smoking, because being against something merely brings you back to it, to release it you would have to love it, love every cigarette as you light it, every one. Only then will you see that it has nothing to give, it can only damage and take from you.

All addictions are examples of distance from source, or moving away from the energy that would heal us, they are the preserve and stamping grounds of the ego-mind of the circle world, they are a very destructive form of intellectual nihilism, as if the ego by its selfish decisions somehow grants us immunity from the negative effects of what we do. As a basic expression of energy they are simple soul denial, they are a teenager shouting and screaming that it's not fair, that energy isn't true, and that's why they are being forced to do whatever it is they do.

To get the true strength that we require for a happy and productive life from the food that we eat, we first have to be a being in balance. We have to start to fix our H.E.F.'s and get the correct energy flows moving through our chakras. When we achieve this, then, and only then, can we begin to understand the foods that our bodies are asking us for. Another thing to remember is that foods have an energy requirement too, they have an energy cost for them to be processed properly for the correct carrying out of their purpose.

We talked earlier about our emotional states affecting the processing and usage of foods; well, here is where we change that, and it should be so easy, we all have access to a wide range of nutritional information these days, what's the problem here? We do not need to feel that we have to change our whole lives to effect real change in our H.E.F.'s, and subsequently this will show in our general well- being. I know that many of us are willing to step on to the energy path, and indeed do read about the subject, but step back from it feeling that it is too high a mountain to climb. So it follows that we have to feel good about eating and the food we eat, at whatever level of wealth or health we are at now.

We have to get a balanced view of food and the life-giving energy that it provides, as well as the nutritional characteristics that we know so well. Many people these days choose to eat a vegetarian diet, leaving meat out of their lives because of their concerns about cruelty to animals. They are also concerned about what they have read about the 'fear energy' that animal protein carries, worrying that they will inherit that fear if they ingest the meat.

There is nothing wrong with making a lifestyle choice like this, and if it feels good do it, but at the same time we need to make sure that we do not then stigmatise those who choose to still eat meat. We mustn't feel that vegetarians are somehow more 'spiritual' than meat-eaters because this is a holier-than-thou approach that denies any benefits of eating meat, and also is another way of dividing people into 'us' and 'them'.

When you move to a higher frequency and fix your H.E.F., you will have the ability to eat meat and use its excellent grounding qualities without becoming the fear aspect, you will be able to negate that effect. There can be just as much fear energy in an addiction that uses substances other than meat as in meat itself. Having said that I feel that red meat is a little too dense, and personally I stop at fish and fowl.

Equally, you mustn't feel that you have to have meat if you don't desire it; there are many alternative vegetable protein alternatives these days. Use your intuition whilst not condemning another's choices; we have to have the freedom and ability to choose what we consume, and not feel that there is a 'bad' or 'not spiritual' component to the choices we make. There is no need for stigma or bad feeling towards another about what they choose to eat, let's not make food choice a political definition of who we are, let our energy do that, and anyway, there's enough of that in the world already.

So how do we balance looking good, because let's face it that's what most diets are really about, feeling good, and more importantly, feeling good about the food that we can afford?

Well, we now know that both internally and externally our physical bodies are a visible and feeling map of the actual state of our H.E.F.'s, through our appearance, manner, and state of grace, or not as the case may be, we can see subtle energy in action or energy and emotion blocked. We know that our mental/emotional programming is very powerful and actually controls the way that our bodies process the food that we eat.

So, if we have begun to change our attitudes towards the energy that we ingest, why do the expected changes take so long, is it because of fear lingering in another form? This is an important point and often I find people have stalled on their paths because of a lack of 'visible' change, they are still the same waist measurement shall we say. Everything feels hard and they think that whenever they move forward that another obstacle is revealed. This is natural, and is also part of the body changing from running on adrenaline and nervous physical energy to actually gaining life energy from the proper digestion and assimilation of their food.

What it reveals, though, is the classic human circle-world problem of needing to be congratulated for small victories, it shows us that even though we are moving past and through the fear about food, we are not making the next step that will propel us forwards, and that is by moving into trust. Fear itself cannot rule all aspects of our personalities, we have other resources, but when fear is joined by its bestest buddy, 'lack of trust', then we are caught in a loop. We have to move into a small clear space where we can feel that we do trust something, maybe just the fact that we are moving through our processes into better energy, but we have to trust something, somewhere, here and now.

I've talked about ego in other chapters of this book, so what part does it play in the fear and 'lack of trust' food and drink disorders? If we look at the way that the huge industry of food and drink, and the many advices offered about the same, in their confusing multitudes, it would be simple to conclude that a lot of people are 'out of control' when it comes to food and drink. So, what then does the wisdom of the diet and the food fads offer us in exchange? Simple, control, and in that one word you can see where the ego is hiding. Conventional food wisdom states that overeating is out of control, and that dieting and limiting intake is in control. How many times have you seen this leader on a magazine or book cover?

"Take back control of your life, with our new 'suck nourishing tide-washed Devon coastal gravel' diet." That's great, but if you accept the 'take back' part of the title, then you immediately concede defeat, yes, you inwardly moan, I am out of control, as you pick up the magazine and walk over to the counter, and here is my salvation, gravel-sucking, ah-well the macrobiotic snail farming was getting a bit much.

Where are the mentions of subtle energy, of soul nutrition, of loving your food, then changing the process of how you look and feel about yourself? They aren't there, and nor will they ever be when the whole circle world of see-sawing weight and bad feeling about food relies on the mental emotional flip-flop of 'out of control' into 'in control'. Here is the cheeky naughty world of the ego tricking us again! You will look and feel better, if, and only if, you do what we tell you, and then you will be in control. But if it doesn't work (because the way we programme the processing of our food hasn't changed yet), then it isn't our fault, synchronise your watches with the atomic clock please, because when we said three successive sucks of two separate pieces of gravel, we meant that they should be exactly fifteen seconds between each suck and at exactly eight minutes after you feel worse than before... We know the story, and how it ends, don't we?

Meanwhile, back at the ranch, where does that leave us? Always struggling and fighting against an invisible foe that doesn't appear to be able to be defeated. But we now know that this is an energy process that can be changed, we know that if we can change the way that we feel about the food that we eat then we can re-educate ourselves about its subtle energy effects.

Each time we approach the consumption of anything with an attitude of depressed or deflated energy, and then we project that thought or feeling into the food as we eat it, then the negative emotional power of the thought is added to the negative way we feel about eating the food. This is double trouble on a large scale that affects us almost immediately after we ingest it, with another negative emotional thought of guilt.

These thoughts combine and then implode in our already beleaguered H.E.F.'s and send a powerful signal to the body; this food is to be processed stressfully, and with all negative implications allowed. You thought it was going to make you fat, off it goes to be adipose; you thought it was going to rot your teeth, cue the acidic deposits; you thought it was going to give you spots, cue the clogged pores and matter deposits, and it goes on, according to our thoughts about it.

Yes of course we need to move through the fears and accept that we need to trust the process a lot more, but because food is so emotive and has such powerful existential issues surrounding it, we have to go a quantum step further, we have to love it. Every morsel and mouthful must be loved and appreciated. To change the energy patterns that we have projected into our food for years we have to go further. It isn't enough to accept it, or to just feel good about it, though that helps a lot, we have to really love it, and that includes everything.

We have to remove all the emotive soubriquets that we attach to our 'treats', like 'I deserve it', 'I earned it', or my personal favourite, 'I'm worth it.' After a bad day and a lot of emotional reacting to other's behaviour, we have to have something to 'feel better', to feel more comfortable, that we have been rewarded for our sterling service against all odds. All of the above lock us into the emotional flip-flop of the circle-world, and by their opposite nature, i.e. rewards that soothe after the awful day endured by the hard done to soul, then we are damning ourselves to the repetition of that cycle, over and over again, as many times as we like.

What has to be changed are our attitudes to the way that we approach food: there are no good foods and there are no bad foods, there are good foods that have gone bad, but that's an issue of care. Look at all the emotive tags we have for different foods, look at the way that we label things as 'good for us' and 'bad for us', in the mistaken thought that wherever those foods are eaten, and by whomever, that the physical effects they will have are just the same. But we go further; we apply these emotive labels to the way that we observe people eating.

What do we think when we see an overweight person tucking into a double-fudge delight ice cream, in Winter, at 10 in the morning, be honest? What do we think when we see a very thin person on the gravel-sucking diet? How about a pregnant woman smoking or an alcoholic homeless person, swigging out a plastic bottle of cider wrapped in a brown paper bag? Are our thoughts supportive, or even sympathetic? No, we judge them as harshly as we judge ourselves, and these judgements carry an energy burden that isn't being dealt with and processed by ours, or their, energy fields.

We are simply storing the energy and bad feelings as excess

baggage, avoirdupois that just won't go away, and harshly critical observations of our food that are really swingeing self recriminations. How about this little phrase allegedly often related to ballet dancers in training;

"Remember students, before you eat, a moment on the lips, a lifetime on the hips!" Can it get any harsher than that? Where is the recovery from that one, all eating is evil, I must eat but it is bad for me? These phrases sound simple but they are not, in fact they carry huge energy charges that have to go somewhere, and we know where that is, don't we?

We must go from this condition and feeling of fear and negative emotion into a calmer space. We have to begin to choose the things we desire to eat because we love them. If we can't love them, then we must at least feel and think that we have chosen them, not that they have chosen, or have power over us.

Here's an exercise to try that will change the energy and programming that we have around food and drink, and indeed any addictions that we nurture and live. Choose something to eat that you like, but it has to be something that you also have negative connotations about too, or something that even though you like, you 'know' is bad for you.

Now decide that you will have some; do whatever it is you do to get it/them, maybe go to the fridge, or the supermarket, wherever. When you buy it you must say to yourself, gently but forcefully too, that *you* are choosing this, *you* are buying it because *you* desire it, not the other way around. Smile as you take it away, and feel happy that you have chosen this thing that you love to have.

When you sit down to eat/drink/smoke whatever it, say out loud, "I love this <insert bad thing here> and I will enjoy this." Hold it and smile at it, love it and appreciate it. Give thanks out loud for the fact that you can enjoy this again. Then get on with it, but take your time, savour every morsel,

chew carefully every mouthful.

When you feel that you have had enough, sit back and consider how wonderful it was that you have had 'it' again, imagine it floating happily as it is being powerfully and properly assimilated, there are no ill effects nor will there be. Then feel happy that you made this wise decision and remind yourself how much you love the 'bad' thing and how good you feel about it. Then relax and sigh a deep and contented sigh.

There is a lot of talk these days of the holistic approach to living and eating, and somebody also punned 'wholistic' which I like, relating to the whole of the person being included in the healing process. Both laudable, and ways that a lot of people are choosing, yet still I have had people asking me why they don't feel complete yet, why there seems to be something missing, what is the last piece of the jigsaw? It's difficult to answer this in a general way, especially after many have spent considerable amounts of money so far in their fruitless quest.

What I think it boils down to is this; no one has told them that before anything can be completely effective in their lives they must have all channels open and be connected above and below with a through path. You guessed it, a fixed and healed H.E.F.

Time spent in communing with the divine connection within us is never wasted, and it doesn't need to be hours at a time, minutes will do. Try this before your next meal or snack, look at the food and thank it for the energy that it is sharing with you, give a nod to subtle energy and thank it for just being here. Simple as that, it will take about thirty seconds to a minute, that's all. If you do this every time you eat or drink for a week, then you will go a long way towards convincing energy that you are sincere and worthy of working with. This works wherever you are, at work, at home, in a restaurant, even in a pub or bar. Doesn't even have to be out loud, you can do it in your head.

When we achieve a balance of energies in our H.E.F.'s and through our chakras, or even, when we start to sincerely move towards this conclusion, then we can begin to access the true energy that we require from the foods that we eat. We need to change the ways that our bodies digest and store and ultimately use the energy components from our foods, and we have to learn and understand that being frightened and judgmental of ourselves and our food, can only end in more negative emotional feelings.

Once we move through fear and lack of trust into balance, we will understand that there are foods with higher energy frequencies and also those with lower frequencies, and that these qualities do not mean 'good' or 'bad'. We will become more confident with our enjoyment of food and drink as we learn to discern and differentiate between what we desire, and what desires us. It is better to eat something 'bad' joyfully, happily and in choosing, than to eat a raw carrot unhappily and resentfully, because we feel that we have to. Not that we should repeatedly choose this, eating the carrot in happiness and thanks is even better than the bad thing, but we have to get to the happy feeling to get the benefits of this effect.

Raising our energies through the H.E.F and happy interaction with the food that we require, will free us from the energy debt of those foods that are supposedly bad for us. I must add though that this isn't a carte blanche to pig yourself at the chocolate shop all day and then pronounce that you are happy! No, you cannot fool subtle energy; it knows the difference between sincere inner attention and paying lip-service to get more of something guilt-free. Remember that first you have to free yourself from guilt to access the H.E.F. anyway, it won't be conned to satisfy negative energy driven greed.

Accessing the higher frequencies of the food that we intake and enjoy, will allow our bodies to assimilate every positive aspect of those foods and allow us to process the true energies of our lives in a better and more wholesome way. We will replace the energy debt of what has eaten at us, and what we are will easily cope with whatever life hurls at us with strength and confidence.

See yourself in that posh restaurant after two happy and chomping courses, and when the waiter returns and asks you, with his lip curled up in a sneer,

"Would you like to see the sweet trolley?" You'll smile broadly and gaze at the trolley, then with an air of confidence you will say,

"I'll have the Crème Brule, with extra chocolate sprinkles please, but no more than that, until tomorrow."

Then breathe out as the other diners gasp as your spoon dives in...

Chapter Two

"Square into Round won't go."
Work-Career.

From an early age we are conditioned to accept the idea that attainment in life is directly linked to what we can earn and achieve through work. This idea is called the 'work ethic' and at its core it is a good idea; that we should work and endeavour to improve our lives is good, but in modern times the pressure of the circle world has changed how we perceive ourselves. Nowadays many of us define ourselves by what we have and what we do, not who we are and what we bring to the world.

Many of us are being boxed up into shapes that we do not like, and have to stay in unfulfilling jobs to service lifestyles that allow us to live beyond our means, thus forcing us to be in servitude to the jobs that we do. The mental push created by the circle world's general stressful attitude towards money and jobs, not helped in the slightest by the doom and gloom-laden media, pulls us away from the soul purpose of our lives and leaves us bereft of positive life-changing energy connections.

If each day brings a step into a work situation that we great with an inner-groan of heartfelt pain, then how are we in service to the universe, how are we in service to our work? The short answer is that we are not, and if this is how we feel on the inside, then we know that it must be impacting the energy that we project to the outside world. I don't want to dwell overly on the negative aspects of work that we don't enjoy, but I feel that it affects a lot of people, in terms of energy and our H.E.F.'s.

There are as many personal stories as there are people on the planet, and they are all unique to us, no one else can really know how we feel and perceive our own world. In relation to work and career though there is a common factor running through all our stories; we all need to feel part of this world and to feel that we are contributing, that 'I make a difference' emotion. When we are in work that we don't like, or that doesn't like us, then we cannot get to that feeling, and the grass on the other side of the street definitely looks greener.

The negative emotion of being trapped or feeling hemmed into a job or career also brings with it the energy or restriction and constriction, we quite literally feel squeezed into this place that we resent so much, and nothing can go right with this simply because of the energy projection that we have created. It is a downward spiral that once begun is not positive in any way.

So how can we change the way that we feel to find the job or career that really fulfils all the basic human and family needs and also fills the soul up with funky fun vibes too? First we need to look at the way that we feel about work, are there any hidden blocks that we need to deal with before we can approach the true path that we desire so much.

Finding the perfect career is more often a case of sorting out our 'now' situation rather than the true path being hidden. There are always clues inside us that point the way to the work that will really service our soul connection, there will be signs and feelings that lean us toward something, whether we consciously acknowledge them or not. The way to greatest happiness usually tends to be through the path of greatest service to the universe, and there are as many different paths and ways as there are people, probably more. What can stop us from finding that 'way' through is the ego's conditioning from within the circle world.

Whilst we have been labouring in the circle world and not finding our true path the ego has not been still. It knows that we feel disappointment and that we feel frustrated, so it cunningly replaces all these little hidden pointers to 'who we really are' with material desires. The ego fills our heads with what we want as a physical outcome, the cars, the houses, the clothes, and on and on. But what it doesn't do is work out how we are going to get to these things through work, it merely tells us repeatedly that we can not be happy until we have these things in our lives.

There is a clear difference between daydreams of riches and a clear and defined desire; the daydreams are always coming from the ego energy of wanting and the clear desire comes from the energy projection of 'I can have this thing in my life.' The ego wants us sitting at a desk miserable and surfing the net for what we can't have, and not striding confidently into a new day knowing that we are bringing to us our desires.

Let's look at the energy of frustrated work; if the negative focus of our day-to-day energy is at our horrible boss/job/career/colleagues/salary (delete where applicable) then we ourselves are adding to that creation and the negative frustration. As we feel worse and worse and project this energy outward in our wrong-thinking, then that cannot come back to us as good or positive energy, and whatever we try to do it will be tainted by that energy. The bad boss's attitude will become worse toward us as they translate the energy of our justified and hurt intransigence as incompetence, laziness, awkwardness and an unwillingness to contribute to the workplace. The very people that 'have it in for us' will find more buttons upon us and many new ways of pushing them, to their delight and our further frustration.

Through our feelings of dislike and frustration we are actually revealing our weaknesses to others and since most of them are in the circle world, then they will revel in having a go at us. When we are often in the energy fields of others then we are also projected at by their fears and frustrations too, in fact their energy is unlikely to be better than ours, unless they have read this book of course, and we become battered by that too. Its unlikely that there will be an entente cordiale in this situation until we back away from the hustle and the bustle and we retract our H.E.F.'s and realise that our energy projections are as much the aggressor as everybody else's.

We have to see that we are all in this together, and that the distance we feel from the people or situations that we dislike so much is not as far as we incorrectly think. Sitting across the room from a boss that we are mentally criticising is no distance at all to our and their energy projections. In every situation like this there is an energy tussle going on, with both parties feeling that the other doesn't know their negative and mean thoughts, when in fact their energy projections are plain and obvious and usually telegraphed by their posture or body language.

Could it be that the chest infection that just won't shift, or the cold that turns into flu, or the headaches that turn into migraines, are not just the random attacks of wicked germs, but they are the accumulated physical effects of the negative energy that we have projected and has been projected at us? Could it not be that all the time signed off work on the sick is an outer expression of an inner feeling that we can't cope, that we can't stand the life that we have created? Why else would we feel under utilised or unappreciated, if we haven't been part of the energy process all along?

The upshot of all this is that we have to fix the energy of the situation before it can improve, without clearing out the closets of all the negativity and bad feeling, then even if we move to another job, that energy and bad feeling will go with us. Whatever changes we make externally, meaning everything to be different 'this time' will catch up and make itself known in very short order. Obviously where we are 'here and now' is who we are right now, and it will continue to affect what we do and feel, until we decide to change it, and no amount of external changing will do that for us, we have to begin it for ourselves.

If we begin to approach the sorting out of our H.E.F.'s then we will at last begin to see what we really feel about the work situation that we are in, right now. At least then we could begin to feel that we aren't 'the problem' and neither is the awkward boss or the job we don't like, we will be able to see that the whole thing is a negative emotional creation that is blocking us from seeing the real way forward. That's the most difficult part of dealing with emotional energy problems, they always hide as other people being the problem, and they most certainly do not want the burden of you taking responsibility for anything. Our egos will always take the path of least resistance and blame others for energy blocks that we can solve, that way we are one step removed from solving the problem and the ego has its 'story' and its pain still intact and fully dysfunctional.

I often mention ego as though it is separate from the 'who' that we really are, and when we are cleared and connected it is, but until then we process most things through the ego. Trouble is we can't just step away from ego and ignore its complaints because we use ego to make decisions, and even after we are cleared we will need to make decisions, so our aim should be to get the ego to work with us and not against us. I've mentioned previously that what ego fears most is its 'death', which is what the ego 'sees' change as, and it will not co-operate easily.

So ego will always try to convince us that we are 'worth' more than we have now, it will talk up our desires and will interpret these desires as jealousy and envy, why should such a person have that car, we are worth more than them, they are this and that and worse, whereas we are holy and good and always smell lovely. Therefore we 'deserve' that more than them, and they've cheated to get that thing, brown-nosing the boss, that's why they get the bonuses and we don't! I'm sure that many of us can recognise all or part of this particular mental loop, it's certainly a favourite of hard-done-to ego's everywhere, and joking aside, it can lead to some awful responses and reactions, we only need to watch the joyful 'news' to see events that come from envy every single day.

What we have forgotten, and of course the ego has forgotten to remind us, is that wherever we are here and now, and whatever we find our situation to be, is simply the result and manifestation of all our previous thoughts and feelings. We are what we have thought and felt before now, in our previous days, hours and minutes. We cannot change a negative now for a positive now with the same mode of thinking and feeling, we have to change into a better way of thinking and feeling 'here and now'. To bring the desired job or career into our lives we have to begin by looking at what we really desire to do and why.

So where do we begin, what is the one thing that we can do that will begin to change things? Well, I'd say that the one greatest thing that we can do to move into energy work and activate our H.E.F.'s is to take responsibility for what we have manifested. Take a moment at your desk, or wherever you are, and breathe in. Disconnect from the frustration or boredom that you feel for the workplace and your colleagues, and if it is just you, then disconnect from that anger at yourself too. Try to stop the mental processes that create the frustration and remember that for whatever reason, at some time in the past, you chose to be here. There may have been reasons that forced that choice, but they too were results of previous manifestations. Once you have managed to pull away from the wrong thinking then try some right thinking. Picture your boss or a troublesome colleague and inwardly smile at them, whatever your beef with them, or whatever they have done to you, acknowledge that they are doing the best that they can, whatever that is. Hold this thought for thirty seconds then let go, and breathe again. I'm not saying that you should instantly love them, but I am saying that you should pull away from your negative thoughts or projections at them, whatever they have done to you.

Taking this responsibility acts to pull all the energy we have invested into the hustles and tussles and the cut and thrust of the workplace. We have to acknowledge that energy work starts with ourselves, and doing the above exercise does just that. Acceptance and forgiveness starts with the self, and removing ourselves from situations that we do not like requires that we release ourselves from the very situations that have held us there. This is a very powerful step and a great move towards a connected and fully-functioning H.E.F.

The other benefit of taking responsibility for our energy and previous manifestations is that it removes us from the need for the approval of others. To really free ourselves from past negative work patterns and to move towards a job or work that we love, we have to release ourselves from the need for the approval of others. We do not need the good opinions of others to create the life that we desire; in fact seeking this approval always results in us giving away the power of choice to those very people. They cannot understand or feel what we truly desire, whatever they say, and they certainly cannot move us towards those desires, especially if they have not cleared their H.E.F.'s. Moving away from this need and the desire to get the nod of approval from family, friends or workplace colleagues is a very powerful giant step into manifesting what we truly desire from the unseen, and bringing it to us all the faster.

One energy concept that some people have difficulty in understanding is that of being in service. In the world of energy and source this is a very simple and powerful concept, but in the circle world of the ego it is always misinterpreted and misrepresented. If I say to you that your way to true happiness lies in service to the universe what picture does this conjure up? Do you instantly bristle, thinking that you will have to become a missionary and give up pizzas? Does it sound like you will not enjoy it, and that all the material benefits of life will have to be given up? Never again will you enjoy cream cakes and red wine?

That's what the circle world wants you to think whenever 'service' is mentioned, it wants you to reject the concept and dismiss any idea that it might work for you. Wait a minute though, is this how service actually is? Has the ego actually looked at what is involved in terms of energy? I think not, why should it, from its perspective there is no need to complicate life by adding things like happiness and fulfilment, is there? The word 'service' also carries connotations of Nuns and Nunneries, Missionary work in far-flung jungles, and other high-faith devotions. What it doesn't say to us is freedom, wealth and happiness with a good old dollop of good health thrown in, but it should.

The greatest service to and for the universe that any one human being can do is to become an effective energy person, to become a discrete and separate, but at the same time loving and caring soul. When your energy field is free of blocks and fear and anger have dissipated, then with your higher energy connections and your healing earth connections you become a transformer, converting high- frequency energy into a baser, slower frequency to heal the earth. Your energy radiates to all around you, allowing them the space for energy freedom in turn. This is the true meaning of energy service to the universe, and that in itself is a great service, and a great higher purpose for all to achieve whilst down here on earth.

So it is true to say that our real life purpose is to be happy, and that to do that in our work, after having cleared and healed our projections, we have to retract inward and begin to examine the 'who' that we are and then we will find the 'what' we want to do with our lives. Everything that has been created in this world has been designed, drawn, manufactured, then distributed, sold and bought by other people, and they all play a part in this world. All we have to do is to find the part inside us that is passionate about the role we want to play. We have to take the time to decide what way we desire to contribute to the all that is, and we need to move away from the gravitas of the negative energy situations that we have recently moved away from.

There is one aspect of the circle world that I must talk to you about here, and that is the pressure to 'do' things as fast as possible. The way that we rush around these days is quite unseemly to energy, and it doesn't allow any time or space for us to properly integrate the energy of change that we have set in motion. When we make big changes we must begin to take the time to allow that change to assimilate in our energy fields and our lives. Instead of belting off to solve the next problem in a flurry of 'doing', why not tell yourself that you will relax and allow this change to register, that there is more than enough time and there is. Ego wants you hurrying about and faffing and huffing and puffing expressly because it doesn't want you to integrate anything at all. Take the time to allow energy changes to heal, and then they will, in time, reveal what you really desire to do.

So, to be in service to the universe we have to start by being in service to ourselves (by fixing our H.E.F.'s) and then we become a service to others, just like that. OK, the road may be long, but you are strong, and he ain't heavy, he's your aura! When your energy is truly your own you can do whatever you desire to do, the choice is entirely yours to make. The problem is that we won't know what we truly desire until we begin to fix our energy, and then the little clues that we always have will become great big neon arrows in the night sky, saying 'this way noodle-head, what are you waiting for!'

I should also mention that there is nothing at all wrong with wealth and the acquisition of said; as with anything in this multi-verse of many things, it is always our intent and desires that shape what comes to us, and then the outcome is changed or altered by what we do with what comes to us. Once we have a complete soul connection then it would prove very difficult indeed to manifest stuff for nefarious purposes, and we wouldn't feel that way about things anyway. Remember all the evil that men (and women) do is always coming from a negative persona that is always the result of a damaged or missing H.E.F, and the lack of a higher or healing connection.

Think of all the great things we could do with wealth, and that this wealth can be gained from doing what we love, and having the happiness of a job well done; well what more could we ask for? All that is required starts with us taking full responsibility for what we have created in our lives, and if that is too hard for you to do right now, then try this; acknowledge to yourself that though you didn't ask for what has happened to you, to your knowledge at least, but that you did play a part in its creation. Even this is a step forward and an acknowledgement of higher energy that cannot fail to have a positive effect in our lives, and in our energy fields.

There is a point where the energy world and the circle world cross and we have to be aware of this in our desires and needs. When we have a desire we have the ability, after some energy work and clearing out of the emotional closets, to manifest it in our lives. Now I am not about to tell you that there are some things that you can't manifest, because that wouldn't be true. What I am going to tell you is that there are some things that wouldn't manifest as you think they will, and that is because of the energy package that you have brought through into this life.

What does this mean to us then, how do we know when we have chosen a desire that crosses into the circle world from the energy world? Imagine that all your life you have desired to be a pop star, a balladeer that people clamour to see. But you can't sing very well, if at all. But you 'know' that you have star quality, if only you had the money for singing lessons with a great vocal teacher. So you start your manifesting path knowing that the stardom you crave is on its way. You work on your H.E.F and the money picks up and you get the lessons, you are in heaven and only ten lessons away from the Royal Albert Hall, or so you think. Then after the fifth lesson, and you have told everybody that you are on your way, the teacher beckons you away from the microphone, and this is what she says;

"Darling, I have to tell you, in all honesty, that you do not have the vocal chords to be a great vocalist, but you do have the ability to be a decent backing singer, and I think we should work on that from now on. However I do admire your devotion and a friend of mine is stage-managing the next 'Whoop-de-hoop-mama' concert, she said that she'll audition you for a backing part, and with a bit more work I think you could do it, what do you say?"

Well, what would you say? Would you sink back into the welcoming arms of false pride and wounded ego, and then scream out of the building demanding your money back and calling the teacher a charlatan whilst shouting that Madonna needs lessons from you? Would you sit there and collapse into fits of righteous sobbing whilst the embarrassed teacher hugs you and says "there, there…"? Or, would you take the true energy path and realise that the universe is doing the most it can right now and throwing you a lifeline, a way into the business that you desire so much? Who knows what might happen once you are in there, but one thing is for certain, you have to get in there first for it to happen in your life.

Can you see what I mean about the energy and circle world crossing? In our deep yearnings we forget that the name of the world that we love is show **business**, and that it has a commercial reality. Yes we can get in, with energy work, and yes we have then a great opportunity, but not every singer can be the lead singer of 'Whoop-de-hoop-mama', and indeed not everybody with the actual ability is cut out for that role. It's always the ego that says 'if you ain't at the top you're nothing' but that is patently untrue, for every pop star that we idolise there are a hundred others in the background doing a myriad of jobs, but at the same time being very involved with the whole business. They are there now, doing it, and if that is where we want to be, then when the universe gives you a bus-ticket get on the bus.

If we sit back on our nicely- padded posteriors and wait for divine intervention, or walk in the park looking for the entrance to Narnia, or for a white-gloved butler to pop out from behind a tree and say 'this way oh sainted one, your perfect life awaits', then we may be waiting and yearning for quite some time.

But if, after making moves to fix our energy, we decide that we can manifest the job that we desire, and that we are willing to do what it takes to get that into our lives, whilst keeping on with the energy work, then I am willing to bet that the universe will work with us and meet us more than half way. I don't think that there is anything in the universe that can guarantee more that you will be moving towards your true desires than fixing your H.E.F. and working with energy. Taking responsibility for your energy and its creations is of paramount importance, and nowhere are its results more obvious than in the world of work and career. You can fix your energy, and you can choose and move towards and into the job or career that you choose, just take the time for the energy changes to integrate, and look for the signs at the crossroads. I wish you all neon signs saying

'THIS WAY FOR JOY AND HAPPINESS!"

Chapter Three

"How are we relating?"

Now let's speak a little about human relationships; you know the ones that drive us nutty most every day? That may be true for most of us, but we can't get away from them, or the fact that they are the core of what we are, and what we are capable of as human beings. The energy of the 'who' that we are now shows in the qualities of our current relationships. All of our hopes, dreams and desires are expressed and lived through other people. Our aspirations and barely- dared spoken hopes are voiced to others, and to their good ministrations we listen in the hope of validation and support. Even when we are in opposition to people we remain tied to what they do and say, and their reactions, until we remove our energy from the conflict.

Why is there so much interpersonal conflict in the world, with family members and friends, lovers and colleagues, acquaintances and strangers? We all have the capability of giving and sharing love, support, kindness and whatever else we may have to give. Surely there are enough people in the world for everybody to work together and be happy, healthy and abundant? Why then can't this happen, why doesn't the circle world move to fix their dilemma? Maybe it is because the doctrine of the circle world is to grab what we can and then fight to keep hold of it. Maybe it is because it doesn't tell us that there could be plenty for all and that all we need do is to create positively and then share.

The same conflict is repeated in our relationships, the same battle to get attention and our own way and to keep it that way occurs in our lives day by day. Family members, friends and lovers batter each other with their learned fears and prejudices that have been taught by the actions of the circle world around them, how could they see things differently? Other people are seen by some to be there to be owned and changed to our way of thinking, not loved and nurtured and set free to be themselves. Love itself is seen by the ego to be fickle and fleeting, owning and smothering, not supportive and giving, freeing and eternal. Small wonder then that many of us wish for relief from the pressure- cooker that families and relationships have become, so we turn outward and look into the circle world hoping to find our answers, but is that where they lie? What is it that causes such trouble and stress, why can't we get on with our people, why can't we find the right people, where do these obstacles and blocks come from?

Here we are on planet Earth, alive and kicking, and what is the most important thing to us? I'm quite sure that the largest parts of our lives are taken up with relationships with human beings and other animals. For most of us it is the quality of our interpersonal relationships that actually creates the way that we feel about ourselves and our relationship with the rest of the world. It is a quality and a requirement of sainthood, to be able to suffer terrible family problems, partner problems, and yet still be able to face a day at work or home with a genuine smile, and how many of us can lay claim to that?

Yet we know now that in terms of energy and our H.E.F.'s that the world and its people greet us from the quality of the energy and emotions that we project. If we are coming from a damaged H.E.F. then how can we expect greater energy than we have now, and if our intentions for the day are higher than the energy that we ourselves possess, then what might happen? Often good intentions take on the energy of misunderstandings, people will misinterpret the hurt way we look as aloof or arrogant, or self-pitying. If at work or school we could have the experience of people talking behind our backs, or they could even attempt to undermine our position.

Damaged social expectations and hurt expressions cannot actually do anything about the fact that we project all of our emotional blocks and prejudices, hurts and pain into the world ahead of us. Our H.E.F. and its energy are at the finishing line before the smile is off the blocks! Why does this happen? What, we think, could be wrong with our smile or our good intentions for the day? Why don't other people get what we are thinking, doesn't that radiate outward from the aforementioned smile? Well I'm sure that it would, if that was all there was to us and our characters; but that isn't all is it? What gets to other people first before the smile has a chance to happen, that's right, our negative thoughts and feelings that we project as energy outward from our H.E.F.'s.

We have to share and exchange the energy feelings and emotions that we have, whether they are positive or negative, it doesn't matter which, we are still impulsed by our inner need for communication with others. We look at, talk to, watch, and judge and criticise, touch and emote towards other people. Even though we are separate physical entities there are always energy exchanges going on between us, even with the people that we encounter but don't know. You could say that our capacity for compassion is controlled and limited by the capacity of our H.E.F.'s to anchor and give out the energy of love and human kindness. It follows then that if our energy fields aren't fixed yet, then we will have a limited capacity to express and feel those emotions from others. In fact we will be interpreting their efforts through a damaged emotional sifting system, and that will keep reporting to us that another is being nasty or secretive, or aggressive, or has bad intentions.

Wherever we go our innate humanity will push us to look for good and kindness, but our faulty H.E.F.'s will insist that the world is a dangerous and loveless place. Love can stare us in the face smiling and we will turn away and grind our teeth at the nerve of some people. The damaged or blocked energy field works in both directions; it limits the quality of what we can receive from others or the universe, and at the same time it faithfully projects how and what we are experiencing outwards into the world. Yet energy is always trying to contact us to get us to engage our H.E.F.'s and use the world of subtle feelings and energy; how many times do we have 'gut feelings' about something that we ignore completely, or at best dismiss lightly? What about past relationships or perhaps colleagues at work that we have clashed with, and afterward we say to others, "You know I always had a bad feeling about them and that deal!" There it was, energy intuition stepping in to save us the bother and the trouble and to guide us gently away from the problem people. Did we listen, and did we trust these deep feelings? Nah, brain thought 'leave it; I can deal with this, no need for silly intuitions.'

Why can't we trust our deeper feelings, what drives us away from the beginnings of a far stronger connection to subtle energy than we have had before? I feel it is because we aren't actually looking for answers that give guidance, we have become accustomed to the stress of 'dealing' with things, that in energy terms remain unresolved long after the logical conclusion of events in our lives. We are always running around and 'putting out fires' that aren't actually fires, they are emotional energy residue and blocks that are hampering us seeing the real reason why the events occur that require us to 'put them out.'

"Everything is relative" stated Albert Einstein, and he was right, the fact that he was talking about physics and I am talking about our relative(s) makes no difference at all. Our families, for better or worse, whatever our lives have been, have shaped the 'who' that we great the rest of the world with. Our 'now' has evolved from our families and what we have experienced with them, indeed the all and everything for a human being doing time on planet Earth is centred on those close to us. For the most part, even if we have negative experiences with them, this

135

shaping is part of the process of becoming a complete human being.

Through childhood and into puberty and them on to adulthood, the experiences that we have create the emotional responses that we have now, and it is the way that we have dealt with all those responses that forges the 'reality' illusion that keeps us away from subtle energy and healing. Family is the place where we start to learn about relationships, and of course assuming that our parents or carers will have had clear and connected H.E.F.'s, then we will have had a painless and fully educational childhood...won't we?

Doesn't always actually quite happen like that though does it? What usually happens is that most of our parents don't know about subtle energy because they haven't been taught about it, what else can they do, where could they get this information from? So, instead they create an imprint of their blocks and fears that they project onto our as yet unformed energy fields; we have blocks before we've even started! No wonder we have the terrible two's! We're shouting, as best we can, "stop projecting this yucky stuff at me already, I'm getting complexes I don't even understand!"

Our young and growing and very impressionable H.E.F.'s are getting hammered by the fear and anger projections of older people, OK they love us too, but it is the fear and blocks that remains and endures for the rest of our lives, unless they are cleared. The greatest challenge of all energy work is the unravelling of our childhoods and the damage created by low frequency energy that we have no way of coping with or understanding at all. Part of life's greater challenge is to unwind all this energy mess and to leave it all behind, to stand in our own energy space and not need the emotional or any other kind of support from parents or family. Easier said than done I know, and I appreciate that some of the pains childhood may have made an impression that still lingers, but that doesn't change the fact that at some point we have to step away from the taint of bad memories and energy. What we have to remember with all our dealings with the past, is that a pain recalled is activating that block or damage in our H.E.F.'s, and that is like playing an old and tired video that we have seen hundreds of times before, and expecting a different or better ending.

Without other people to relate to we can lose perspective and direction, and perhaps a lack of parental guidance has shaped and hurt our persona into adulthood. When this kind of damage is carried forward without being cleared or healed it taints all the good energy that is trying to get to us, because a block that is still painful and active can still filter all the good out of anything, even loving thoughts or feelings. The hardest thing to understand when a life is controlled by blocks of a painful emotional nature is that they are completely running our lives, and they are hidden to us. It's like a computer virus hiding in the background and changing all the good that we are trying to do, and misinterpreting all the subtle energy that wants to get to and heal us. Until that virus is removed then we are powerless to see its effects.

When we clear our H.E.F.'s and re-connect to subtle energy, we can remove all of these emotional blocks, but often we are in a mental and psychological loop of not being able to receive the positive benefits of that experience, and we then repeat the behaviour that held the block in place all this time. This is often because the people that created the blocks within us will resist our moving towards healing, coming from their own emotional blocks and pain they resist our healing that moves us away from the behaviour that kept us at that place of hurt. When parents have energy blocks that have damaged their children, then they do not see bad behaviour in its true light, often they will not discourage the negative behaviours, drinking or smoking say, because it validates their pain. The last thing negative energy and emotional pain wants is to be revealed in the light of healing, remember the ego sees change as a small death, therefore it resists all positive change, even encouraging the negative behaviour, saying that 'it hasn't hurt them' and that 'it has made us who we are.'

One of the greatest and hardest (at first) lessons to learn about energy work, is that as our energy rises and we become healed and whole again, that we may have to leave some people behind us. Of course we let them go with love, but we may have to let them go. This can mean moving physically, or just emotionally and mentally, often a combination of all three. We will find just how far they are behind us if we try to convince them of the virtues of our 'new way of life', we may see a side of friends and family that isn't pleasant. Even when we are supported by friends and family, we soon will learn not to respond, or help people as much as we thought we would when first we embarked on this quest.

We will have to learn to pull away from others' energy problems and not be pulled into the emotional mess that they project. Too many times in the past, usually in the name of family or friendship, we will have been pulled into the mire of others' emotional problems and needs for support, so much so that often we find it hard to see where 'we' are and another's problems start. As we slowly begin to return to source energy and build up our energy fields we will have to learn to discern, choosing when to engage and when not to. Often 'not to' will be the best choice, we do not have to stand in another's toxic aura whilst they bemoan the price of cheese and how the universe is out to get them, and then splurge us with their emotional energy and its mucus laden muck.

It is one of the great paradoxes of our action -riddled lives that the greatest gift one can return to the planet is to heal you, and let everybody else be. Just by having a higher vibe you can help all others that you encounter, if they want to be helped, and you don't even have to mention it to them, it just happens. That is a wonder of energy work, but you have to let it happen, if you 'try' to intervene, then you will have that energy burden upon you, and somehow you will have to clear it, and that isn't nice. Better to back away and heal privately for a while, because one thing is for sure, once you have re-connected to higher-energy and the healing source, you will re-evaluate all your relationships, and see them for what they truly are, for better or for worse.

As energy workers in human bodies in charge of our immortal souls progress, people for short, we have to learn that the 'all that is' is us, that above the Earth level we are all part of the same soul force. We are little pieces of the greatness that is source energy, we are at once alone and yet surrounded by love, no, enveloped in love. Source energy is growing and learning about itself through our efforts, and through our relationships, both with others and with source itself. We are alone so that we can learn about and appreciate others and grow through our relationships with them; we have to learn to refine ourselves and our reactions to the world that we have created through previous actions and reactions. In truth there is no alone, at least not when we are connected to energy through our working and healed H.E.F.'s, then we will always feel gratitude and connection no matter where we are or what we are doing.

Alone is simply a description of disconnection from source, as is ego, they are both what happens when we are far from our soul's connection, from the healing force of the planet that we walk every day. It often strikes me as funny and ironic that in Beverly Hills US of A, which area is perhaps the greatest physical embodiment of wealth and ego and separateness on this planet, that nobody walks, they all drive, and if you are caught walking then you are given a ride downtown pronto. They do not touch the planet, nor go through the embarrassment of walking, how removed can you get?

Our direct experiences of love relationships usually start in mid to late teenage, and as we all know, this is a fraught time to try to understand the wants and needs of another when we are struggling to understand our own. The feelings that we go through are often infatuations and obsessions that come from our own direct energy problems that we have transferred from childhood into puberty. Both tribal and loner, intensely social but feeling alone, we often experience real emotional pain as teenagers, and hurt that feels physical as we are rejected by our own idealised obsessions with unappreciative others.

We put all our needs and projected desires for completeness into a desperate search for the ideal person, the one, that we will call girlfriend or boyfriend. In energy terms the ego is rampant at this awkward time; what we as teenagers interpret as 'real' is often self-obsessed and narcissistic, driven by the search for completion through the love of another. But there isn't the emotional sophistication of later life, so these expressions of 'love' are physical, overt and outward.

As teenagers our energy fields are waiting to expand and grow, but they are forced by behaviour to concentrate on just a few areas; the third eye, the heart, and of course, mainly the sacral, or sexual chakra. The focus on physical activities as being 'love' creates an energy roller-coaster that demands to be fulfilled, if we are not with the significant other we are thinking about them, or texting them, or thinking about the next 'love' should this one fail. Contrary to others' opinions, I do not accept that teenagers suffer from lack of self-worth, no, in energy terms I would call it 'lack of the exact type of personal attention that I want right now!' The clamour for so many voices for attention from the chosen peer group is immense and very focussed, I have yet to meet a teenager with a calm and rested energy field, but that doesn't mean that it isn't possible.

There isn't an easy energy way through teenage, it is a necessary forge to get us ready for the pressure -cooker that is adult life, but it would be great if a few teenagers would read this book and become aware of their energy fields, even better do something about them. Then they would improve their lives and they would avoid taking all the mistakes of teenage years into their adult lives.

As we progress into adulthood our desires and needs become more complex, as do our habits. We begin to create a system of things that we do for work and recreation that we think of as being our 'character' or as expressed physically, our 'lifestyles'. We build a mental checklist of physical characteristics that the 'one' would have, and what 'they' would be like, and also we construct mental and emotional images of what 'they' will do with us.

In energy terms what we have forgotten is that being in a close personal relationship with another person is a very complex energy situation. Just as we bring the emotional energy baggage from our lives so far, so do they, and let's not forget that they have their physical and emotional checklists too. Emotionally and physically we try our best to meld our energy fields with theirs, and not always with great success. We find ourselves meeting our own energy field blocks as obstacles or resistance from the dearest loved one, and we mirror our fears onto them, trying to imprint in their heart chakras an image of us from which they can never stray. Some of us even try to change what the significant others are, preferring our own estimation of who and what they should be to their own.

Predictably this ends in painful argument and splits as the 'one' rapidly becomes the 'gone'. These things happen because all the mental estimations of what we desire and what others should be are coming from an energy field that cannot properly process 'love' far less remove the blocks that stop us from reaching the core worth of our partners, and by association, ourselves too. Negative energy that has never been purged from our auras will always result in conflict and argument because that is its nature, it is negative, but the downside of this is that we then believe that relationships are actually about this conflict, that they should be that way.

You know what's coming next don't you? Yes, the conflict will not end until we clear and re-activate our H.E.F.'s, we have to step back from ego and its attempts to control others emotionally, to bind them to us. That is the truth behind the great little statement that says 'If you love someone, set them free.' I often think this is interpreted to mean that you have to leave them, but I don't feel that it means that at all. What it means, as energy, is set them free from your tyranny, sort out your problems, fix your aura, then see what that relationship can become. Better that than be like the wicked queen in Snow White; driven to destroy the beauty that she so admires and desires she mixes a dreadful concoction of fears, hopes, desires, anger and unrequited self-love to poison, or control, the object of desire, and we label this 'love'.

Even if we chose a person from the far ends of the earth, the emotional patterns that are the blocks in our H.E.F.'s will still prevail upon that relationship. However many times we start again, give it another go, or run away to find love elsewhere, nothing will change until we can remove the witches' brew that we project. Heartbreak after heartbreak, argument after argument, and unlike tears in the rain, they won't wash away, these same patterns will come back again and again, until we clear our H.E.F.'s and drop the comedy act that we call 'poor me', only when we are healed and connected can we find that which we seek so ardently, and even then it might still take some work.

But it can be done, we can find the 'right' person, we can have the perfect relationship filled with everything that you desire, but we have to start somewhere, and whatever state our relationships are in now, we have to start now. The onus is on us, we are the ones that have to change for our relationships to improve, for the love of our lives to enter, or even to leave. It is only when we can release all that has gone before, all the disappointments and pain, all the tears on our pillows, all the triumphs at the downfall of another, our despair at our own downfalls. All these things that leave us clinging to a few fleeting moments drifting in the wind of our emotional past, it is only then that we can begin to really feel who we really are emotionally. The one way that is truly effective at releasing all the pent-up and physically stored emotional pain from the past is to blast through them with the energy of source and the cleansing soul-burnishing power of the Earth's energy.

We owe it to our souls to take stock of our lives, we will remember all that has been but without the energy pain-memories that have felt so real, and to agree that we can let everybody else go, we can release ourselves from the need for the good opinion of others and finally be the 'us' that we deserve. Once our H.E.F.'s are cleared and working and we are purged, then the true energy of love can flow through us and affect out lives positively. Only then can we truly see the power of who and what we are; when we move past forgiveness and into allowing another to be, we naturally leave space in front of them for them to step into and improve their lives. Always guiding but never pointing, we shepherd ourselves into a position that love can come to and greet us on our terms. As soon as we are clear and allow the space for love to move in, then it will happily join us, and stay with us, and we can let it be as we are, in love. This is written beautifully in the sage words of Eric Clapton from the song 'Let it grow.'

'Let it grow, let it grow, plant your love and let it grow, in the sun the rain the snow, love is lovely, plant your love and let it grow.'

Indeed.

Chapter Four

'Abundance and Money.'

"Money, money, money, all the things I could do, if I had a little money, it's a rich man's world..."

We all know this famous pop ditty and apologies to Abba, but these lyrics accurately describe the energy cycle that we end up trapped in if we believe the circle world's version of wealth and finance. I feel a considerable amount of us do believe the sentiments that Benny and Bjorn wrote about, no matter how much we talk the talk, there's always that feeling that we need good luck, that the money odds are stacked against us. How are we going to keep our heads above water if the rich are getting richer and the poor are getting poorer?

OK, I'm clichéd out for the moment, and I'm sure that we'll all come to the point in our lives where all the spiritual stuff that we do is trying to sort the money out; it may not even be for ourselves, maybe for a spiritual cause or a business idea. Money is the area that catches us out time and time again, that's why there are so many books available about sorting wealth and abundance out, that's why we buy them all.

So it's probably safe for me to say that we are quite used to the spiritual notion that abundance is but a quick side-step of the mind away from us, that the law of attraction is sat just around the corner with our suitcases of cash, and that all we have to do is wish for, or desire it, and there it is, alakazam bam boom, in our living room! Perhaps some of us have tried the 'relax and wait' method? Perhaps we are very relaxed now, but still waiting, patiently, waiting?

<<Ahem>> (This is just for the waiting ones, all you millionaires at the back skip a few paragraphs, my friends need to know why they're still waiting, OK?)

So why is it then, why hasn't abundance worked for some, and yet it has for others? Are we Karmic criminals, were we part of Ali Baba's crew way back when, was his press wrong, did he have millions of thieves instead of forty? We need to know, and now, this money is a pressure, debts won't wait till next year, mouths need to be fed, mortgages paid, we know the score, so let's get a move on money.

So as much as we try to spiritually relax about money and get our heads around the idea that abundance is there for us too, we are still firmly grasped by the ego running around doing its Chicken Licken dance again, hello circle world, we're back in lack! Adding insult to penury, the more we strive in life, the more money appears to slip out of our grasp like sand sifting away through a grasping fist. Why does it have to be so, what can we do to change this, surely we all desire to accept the concept and therefore make money work for us?

This is a shining example of the circle world in full and effective action, we are sold fear and lack and loss and horror day after day by a media greedy in its need to tell us the horrible and gory 'truth.' We in turn react and create more fear within us and the belief that it's just too hard to do this and win. That's the ego in action, but the real problem is that all this fear is programming the energy of how we feel about money, all the time.

Could I suggest that the basis of these negative money thoughts and feelings have been impressed on us and ingrained into us since birth? Also that the reason why changing our thoughts won't shift our negative money energy implants immediately, is that it is simply thought, and thought doesn't have the 'realness' that feelings have. Those feelings, however negative, are a direct result of how we feel about money. Whatever we think now, the old ingrained feelings remain and come back to haunt us, because they have been projected at us since birth.

Were we taught that abundance is unlimited, that there is more than enough money for everyone, and that it won't run out, nor will the planet's abundance? Not many of us will have had the benefit of that, and it isn't our parents' fault because they weren't given this information either, so they probably thought that they were teaching us 'common sense' when in fact they were teaching us fear about money, about the 'reality' of lack and loss and not having. So our state of thought is just that, thought. It isn't the way that we really feel; yes it can guide and change how we feel emotionally now, but it can't change the ingrained energy that is clogging and blocking up our H.E.F.'s and keeping us from the bags of cash that are just around the corner, waiting.

Look at how powerful money, or abundance, is in our lives; it is how we identify ourselves in the circle world, it is how we experience the rich cornucopia that the world has to offer, it is what we can, or can't buy. Whether it is cars or houses, or clothes and jewellery, there is nowhere else in the circle world that defines who we are to others more than our material possessions.

This creates a dichotomy in our energy fields, a split between material desires and spiritual aspirations; because it seems to us that the circle world is just for capitalists. What then is there for the person that cares about their soul development and energy connections? Are we doomed to poverty and fighting envy, but feeling spiritually superior? The Bible even says that 'it is easier for a camel to pass through the eye of a needle than it is for a rich man to get into heaven...' Thus justifying poverty as 'holy' and adding a dose of negative ego for good measure.

What chance do we have of sorting this little lot out then; on the one hand we have the unholy capitalists that 'have it all', and on the other we have the 'holier than thou' have-nots, and in the middle we have all the ordinary people that are cast between pillar and post, damned if you do and damned if you don't! The simple answer is that these are all systems of control that work by confusing us, and they do work too. Long term they can cause tremendous 'lack of' problems. I think that Janis Joplin had the spiritual/material conflict just right when she sang this little ditty,

"Oh Lord won't you buy me a Mercedes Benz, my friends all have Porsches and I must make amends, so Lord won't you buy me a Mercedes Benz?
Worked hard all my lifetime, no help from my friends, so Lord won't you buy me a Mercedes Benz?"

The circle world is always working its cycles of boom and bust, and this reflects in our own views of what we do with the money that we have, like Pavlov's dogs we react to the latest doom-laden news from the ego-driven media. We are shown extremes of wealth and poverty juxtaposed against what we 'should' be feeling; we cower inside as the 'credit crunch bites' and 'global warming spreads' and the 'stock markets plummet'. I'm waiting for the shock headline;

'...man dies after long and happy life, his kids are all well and loved him, he made a massive contribution to the world and left a handsome legacy, and nobody had anything bad to say about him.'

I'm not holding my breath...

All this doom and gloom pushes us away from spiritual and energy solutions and makes us grab for what we can, whilst we can, we see time and opportunity as limited and closing in, we breathe the dogma of lack. This is how the circle world keeps us away from the *feelings* of abundance and wealth, because whilst all our waking time is taken up with *thoughts* of fear and lack, there is simply no energy space for good feelings.

The last thing that the circle world wants is us feeling wealthy and abundant and ignoring the latest media spin. No, it needs us doing the knee-jerk reactions of shock and horror, or even better, us feeling that we can't have wealth and that abundance just doesn't exist. The worse we feel about money, the worse things seem to get, because negative energy cannot become positive unless it is transmuted into the Earth, thus the whole negative money energy becomes a self-fulfilling prophecy that results in misery and despondence.

What the ego-driven circle world has created in us is the idea that money is a thing, and that it somehow has characteristics that can make it good or evil, that it goes to some people and not others, whom it punishes or rewards, that it goes to itself and away from those that hath not. None of this is true. Money itself is just marked metal and paper; put a fifty on the table and what does it do? Nothing, but what does it evoke in us, apart from the intense desire to grab it? We instantly have mental images of where it might be spent or saved, the bills it might pay. There are many things that just the sight of a brightly- coloured piece of paper can evoke, and that is the magnitude of the power that we grant money.

What money 'is' really is the physical representation of what we can do with it, the experiences that we can exchange it for. We should have no emotional attachment to it at all, but just see that it gives us choices. This is going swimmingly isn't it, what a neat and easy- to- follow little explanation. Now we are seeing our fifty in a whole new light! We are free and it can serve us instead of us being in thrall to it. Hang on a moment though; ego has been listening to all this too. Suddenly childhood thunders back into the room, 'money doesn't grow on trees, you know', you shudder as you reach for the money, eager to hide it away, then the trump card, 'I'm not made of money, you know'. That does it, the fifty disappears into your wallet or purse, and all notions of abundance fly out of the window, we curl around the fifty and whisper,

"It's ours precious, it is ours, just ours."

OK I'm exaggerating but it's not that far from the truth, and it's the same with possessions, they end up controlling us, unless we can change how we feel about them. So if we do desire both wealth and spiritual connection, and both in balance please, then first we must look at our attitudes and feelings about abundance before we examine money itself. Yes coins and notes, or a credit line are a medium of exchange that bring immediate ownership of stuff, but abundance is the means to do everything that we desire, and it has no limits, nor does it ever end, it can't end. Cash itself, as we have seen, carries the energy of how we feel about it, and how we have been conditioned and conditioned ourselves. So, approaching abundance openly and with a good heart, that is willing to accept that the past has controlled us, will allow us to free ourselves from those energy blocks. If we could see money as energy before it gets to us in physical form, and hold that vision, then, and only then, we can change our ideas and feelings about abundance and wealth, so that they can change the way they feel about us too.

Abundance exists at all times, it cannot be switched on or off, it just 'is', flowing a constant flow from above to us down below. It has no emotion about us or as to where it goes, and money has no judgement on us or bad feelings about us. Simple fact is that we have to work hard to block it, and that, my friends, we do. We have moved away from abundance and connection to its benef-icent flow, we have allowed our H.E.F.'s to become in disrepair, we have walked away around the corner, away from our bags of cash. We code the wealth that tries to get to us with the frequency of where we are at now, with all the negatives that we feel about it. If we are acting like Charlie Bucket feverishly searching for the last of Willie Wonka's Golden tickets, then abundance will play our game too and keep hiding the golden ticket that it has for all of us, and this will keep happening as long as we feel the way that we do, until of course, we ask for it back, and now.

It will have become patently clear now that to create the wealth and abundance that we desire in our lives, that we are going to have to continue our starting somewhere, and change the way that we feel about money and wealth and the abundance that fills the energy world around us. We will have to work on the little things that defeat our hopes, the sneaky thought patterns that pop up in our heads unprompted but right on time, time after time.

So let's take a look at these cheating patterns and how they work, come with me on an imaginary troll through a city centre and let's see what happens and, more importantly, why. Here we are then walking downtown, and we notice somebody pull up in a brand new Lamborghini. We would love one of those cars, *but at the moment they are light years away from us.* There it is, right there, the first cheat! We can't have that car, abundance denied, poverty claimed. Then what happens next, do we cancel that thought with a positive affirmation like, *I'm going to have one of those cars one day!* No, what do we follow this with? *Poser,* or, *Why do they deserve that car, must be a criminal!* More lack, followed by jealousy and envy. Tell me, how can abundance step into this energy space? It can't can it, because these thoughts got there first, and they are still active, until we counter them and change how we feel.

We have to move to a different emotional standpoint, and straight away too, these self-defeating thoughts serve only to re-activate the negative patterns that we already have operating in our H.E.F.'s, thus leaving us empty and bitter. It's not just cars either, you could transpose the same situation to include another's clothes, house, watch, body, aeroplanes, girlfriends, boyfriends, friends, and the list goes ever on. I do realise that this is a tough turnaround, but it has to be done, this is the starting point for re-joining with source and the healing energy of the Earth. Why? Because all these thoughts, and the negative feelings that follow them, define *lack* in our H.E.F.'s, and even worse they reinforce the *fact* that we have not got.

What you need to think to turn these energy patterns around are positive thoughts that have no emotional attachment to the thing itself, like these:

'Isn't it great that the universe has blessed that person with that car, surely it will bless me the same too?' 'Wow, they look good in that great car, I'll look that good too when I get mine!' 'What a great car; I'm sure that I could afford one of those if I desired one.'

Smile when you think these powerful positive affirmations, and ignore the nagging voice that says they are silly, that is ego trying to reclaim the energy space. The previous negative thoughts that felt they were so safe roosting in your head will now be ousted, and that is no bad thing. There you go, a positive energy and feeling change in mere seconds, and you don't need to say anything, it costs nothing, nor need you be standing on your head at dawn and wearing a hula skirt. When you first start to use positive affirmations like the above, and feel free to make up your own, you may feel a little phoney, that this energy stuff isn't real... Immediately you should be alerted to the power of the negative affirmations that you have just ousted, look, they are not going without a scrap! So ignore those thoughts and make that mind space our own. What these negative thoughts show us is that we have changed, even in so short a time, we have made a difference to our energy, and put distance between us and the negative. It will shout that 'you can't leave!' but just smile back and waltz off into the sunset, I say, and don't look back.

It is very necessary to overcome the negative programming that the circle world and ourselves have put in place in our energy fields. Each time we manage to reverse a negative thought with a positive affirmation, we create a little more distance from it and create an energy space of our own, that can be filled with positive feelings and therefore energy. When we make continuous effort to do this then we are taking back control of our soul connections and our very lives. But make no mistake, the negative thoughts want us back, and they want us firmly back in the loop of the ego-driven circle world. So for a while we are going to have to work hard and keep the pressure up on monitoring our thoughts. Surely it follows that it won't be that long before we are back in control of our own abundance.

I often mention the circle world, and I'll take a second to re-iterate it here, because nowhere is the circle world more evident than in the realms of abundance and wealth. When an immortal soul in a human body is cut off from higher source energy and from the healing power of the Earth because of a damaged Human Energy Field, then the energy that is trapped in their H.E.F.'s becomes stagnant and negative. What energy there is cannot flow, grow, or be transmuted or renewed as it should be by the natural action of the H.E.F. This condemns people to repeat negative thoughts and actions again and again, without knowing why the same horrible stuff happens to them again and again. Owning a H.E.F. and managing our connections are a great soul responsibility that the people on Earth need to be taking very seriously, and soon.

Let's take a look at how one of these stagnant negative energy loops might work with a little scenario;

It's payday woo-hoo! Her overdraft has dropped to half what it was and she is feeling flush. No, it's more than that; she has worked and slaved over a hot office all week, and put up with all the other nutters and their bizarre behaviour. She does a job she doesn't like, but it

pays the bills, and she's got a shiny new credit card. 'What the heck'
she thinks, looking greedily at the card, 'It'll sort itself out, and I
might win the lottery this week!' 'C'mon' she shouts to office chum,
'we're going to Expensivo's pizza and it's on me!' Chum tags along
gladly, smirking at flush girl. Two expensive pizzas later the bill
thumps on the table, she cringes, but no, she deserves it! 'Friend'
badgers off fatter and money in pocket still. Instead of cutting her
losses and going home she heads for a troll through the mall. Ten
minutes later 'that' bag and 'those' shoes and 'this' dress are firmly
in designer carrier bags around her shoulder. Finally she gets the
train home and stomps though her door crying 'I deserve it!' Door
won't open, bills are wedging it shut, so she pushes harder and falls
in a heap, cushioned by her new purchases. She looks at the bills and
knows that she hasn't got the cash to pay them; head hangs low,
heart hangs heavy, a tear falls down her cheek, 'what have I done to
deserve this, I deserve better!' She finds the credit card and stomps
out of the door and on outward to the off licence.

I'm sure that we can recognise some of these traits and her
negative feelings, coming as they do from the kind of desperation that the circle world injects into us. It's a shame that the
lady in the example couldn't have been taught to recognise these
patterns for what they really were: guilt. The energy of guilt is a
powerful force and it is the opposite of feeling good and being in
abundance. It may seem strange to you me saying that over-
spending and profligacy come from guilt, but they do. Without
knowing it we feel the echo of energy that isn't in our H.E.F.'s i.e.
abundance. The feeling reminds us that we aren't doing the right
thing, and it makes us feel uneasy because we don't yet know
about energy or the reason why. Thus it is easy for the ego to step
in and push us in the wrong direction, so we continue to spend
even though we know that we should stop. The same thing
happens with addictions too.

A powerful reversal is required here and fortunately for us

there is one, and it isn't difficult to do, though it may seem a little odd at first. Money isn't just a form of exchange, it is also energy too, and it carries the energy that we are here and now. We imprint the money that we have and use with our feelings now, this includes credit cards too, and cheques, or internet transfers, however we use and touch money. So the money that we spend from a negative viewpoint carries that energy away from us as it is spent, so that money energy leaves us and has no way to come back to us, the abundant path is blocked. Our energy is depleted by the loss that we feel and no energy replaces it, so no more money can follow it, our wealth is blocked. The object that we buy also has this energy as its signature; it's a very negative cycle that feeds upon itself, until changed, of course.

Frankly this negative cycle needs to be turned around; and it is obvious that this state has come from feelings and thoughts of lack and having nothing or losing things and thoughts of 'not having'. We have to program ourselves with the opposite of fear and lack, and that energy is love, pure and unadulterated love. That's right we have to love every penny that we have or comes through our hands. We have to change the negative energy of fear to a 'knowing' that we do have, and will have again, because we are abundance, we 'are' that energy. We must get back into a pattern of thinking abundantly and every time we spend money we have to feel happy about it. We must be sure in the knowledge that this purchase is worthwhile, certain that our happiness guarantees that this money will return to us soon, and make sure that it has purpose in our lives, or at least really enjoy it and feel good about it, this goes for everything. Even if we spend on a negative thing, to stop the addiction controlling us we have to love it, love spending it, love having it, love using it. This is how we can turn guilt around.

The same goes for bills and the debts that annoy us so much. The annoyance itself is a negative energy that drains us and stops us from seeing the fiscal and energy truth about the matter. We must begin to feel good about the services that we pay for, thank the universe for the use of them, and be thankful and grateful that we were given the credit line in the first place. If we do this then the money we spend carries the energy of love and gratitude, thus allowing that freeing energy to come back to us.

Wherever we come across money in our lives we have to feel good about it, and be thankful for it, even if it comes in the form of an overdraft, be grateful that service was given to us, even if we pay for it, especially if we pay for it. Go over every debt or bill that you have and take responsibility for it; 'Thank you, I created this, thank you for this, thank you for everything in my life that I have created, thank you.' Using these techniques we can systematically remove all of the negative energy frequencies and patterns that have beleaguered our lives, but that we have put in place.

Working positively like this and using positive affirmations and the power of gratitude and love we will begin to reverse the negative energy patterns that block abundance and energy in our lives almost immediately. We will be able to step into a better and more supportive financial energy space sooner than we think, and step powerfully away from the clutches of the circle world of the ego.

I'm counting and projecting seven- figure sums at all of you, and wishing that you are in happiness and loving it, and are thankful every minute of your lives.

I'll end this chapter with a fitting quote from Pink Floyd's track *Money*.

"I'm in the high-fidelity first class travelling set, and I think I'll buy me a Lear Jet!"

Amen to that brothers and sisters.

Chapter Five

Working with Energy.

All through this book I have been talking to you about working authentically with subtle energy through our reconnection to source energy and to the grounding and healing Earth energy, thus allowing us to fix our H.E.F.'s and thus truly beginning our lives. I have spoken about the basics of energy work using our H.E.F.'s and chakras to truly understand why we react the way we do and continue to create problems for ourselves. But (I know what you are thinking) how does this translate practically in our lives now? Do we have to do Yoga at Dawn whilst whistling Dixie and considering the Lily?

Well if it works for you, go for it, but the answer is no, we don't have to do anything like that, unless we want to of course. Working with subtle energy, *'Energy Working'* is available to all of us and at all times. It is never switched off, and there are no membership requirements or funny handshakes. There is no need to buy anything (other than this book) and we are all worthy, yes we are! The only thing that is required is that we recognise and accept that our Human Energy Fields need to be healed and reconnected, and that we accept, allow and begin to receive that joyful and divine connection.

The other main thing that we have to change is how we react to external events and our own internal habitual impulses. Now that we have come to know that all those little niggles that build up during the day, are created from our own energy blocks and incorrect energy projections, and that they have to be released and grounded to Earth to dissipate. Just stopping our inner emotional reactions to these events, and accepting responsibility for them, without reacting to that realisation, is enough to powerfully begin the ball rolling and moving toward healing our chakras and auras. We have to change from beings of reaction and disappointment to beings that are consciously creating our lives with an unshakeable core trust in the universe, no matter what is going on around us.

Finally, we understand that negative energy cannot change its nature, it can only be transmuted into the Earth through a working H.E.F, so we can only begin to change things when we take responsibility for what we have inadvertently created and start to create positively using the amazing abilities of our H.E.F.'s. When we do use positive and loving and supportive energy to change, then, over time, this energy will accumulate and change our life experiences around for the better.

The circle world of the ego requires us to be negatively reactive beings for its continuing existence in our lives. As long as our immortal souls living human lives are reactive and have disconnected and damaged H.E.F.'s then the ego and the circle world will happily control us and direct our lives negatively. Note that the circle world knows about the H.E.F., but it needs our energy and us in existential pain for its continued dominance, so it's not about to tell us about the healing methods, is it?

Now, more than ever before, the progress of humanity depends on more people becoming self-realised and taking control of their own H.E.F.'s. It is time that we all choose to co-create our lives with source and with each other. Conflict can only create more conflict, and comes from conflict. It is time that we choose to create and use our own positive, loving and creative energy for ourselves. Yes it sounds selfish, which would appear to be opposed to 'spiritual' goals, but it isn't at all.

Let me explain: Until our H.E.F.'s are reconnected and our chakras are cleared of energy blocks and miasms, then we cannot get to, or even understand, who we really are. It is only when we 'selfishly' devote ourselves to the reconnection and clearing of our energy that we can become truly effective beings and positive energy creators in the circle world. Then we become able to help others simply by giving them the free energy space, without our projections, to move into. This is a great gift for another person and anyone else that passes close to our energy fields and is very far from being selfish.

To become a fully-realised and aware human being, in the truth of who we really are, with a fully-healed and working energy field, should be the primary aim of all of us. It may seem like a great deal of effort and hassle to do, but the energy reality of it is that all we need to do is to drop all the circle world ego-driven pretences that have held us in thrall for so long. Simply admitting to our inner-selves the deep truth in this, and feeling even an inkling of trust in the process and the greater intelligence of subtle energy, always guarantees a positive response from the universe. The situations and events of our lives will begin to present themselves to us with visible choices, we will 'know' and 'see' the energy way, or the other way. It's easy, we choose the energy way or the reactive way; connection and healing, or eternal waiting and more emotional pain.

Once we have moved onto the energy path, and we have chosen that we would like our Human Energy Fields to be fixed about now thank you very much; then we need to know about the ways that we have to act to increase the flow of subtle and positive energy to us. I know that you want to know the specifics of what to do; well I've included them at the end of this chapter, so you'll have to wait a wee while. Until then, let's chat about the states of being that we can easily achieve that will help us sort out our reconnection and our H.E.F.'s.

Gratitude
OK, the basic energy deal that works well for us down here on planet Earth, is that we have to be grateful for everything in our lives, whatever that may be. Even the bad stuff and I am sorry if

this is very difficult for some of us, even the very bad stuff. The reason for gratitude for the bad stuff is so that we can free ourselves from the energy effects of the events that have occurred in our lives. If we haven't released the need to constantly replay the pain of our lives, then this energy becomes our 'story' and will control what we can manifest for ourselves. It quite literally holds us in an energy loop of re-experiencing whatever that pain was, or is.

Taking responsibility for everything through being grateful for the experience happening works to free us from that pain bondage and allow us to move on. There can be no space in our lives for better, happier, more peaceful energy to move into if we are bearing energy grudges against any person, group or thing? The more time and energy we take to dwell and think negatively about 'bad' things, the more energy and space within our H.E.F.'s we grant to those things. We can talk, and think, all we like about 'letting go' or 'moving on', but these words and thoughts are empty if we are still replaying the pain within us. Then all we are doing is begging for the right to be more miserable about the dreadful stuff that has happened to us, which is pointless, because that right has always been ours, and the ability to choose it, or not, too.

Emotional misery and pain is a conscious act of negative creation that is ongoing and active within our energy fields. It is underpinned and reinforced by the 'poor me' quality of the circle world, and its quality is negative. No matter how much others validate our victim status, even if a million people agree that we are an authentic and 'to be pitied' victim, and that 'it wasn't fair', not one of those thoughts could change the event and move our lives into positive and loving creation. In energy truth, too many of these 'not fair' thoughts and wishes would end up with us being firmly held in the clutches of the circle world of the ego and negative energy creation.

Gratitude changes negative events and their energy because it removes the need for there being a reason for it to happen. If we can accept that the reason was based in a powerful and positive creation, that we may not understand, but we take responsibility for and accept, then we remove the need for its effects to happen again, and we remove the need for any more events like it to happen again. We use the act of gratitude to remove any negative emotional or energy attachments to the event, and to stop it from replaying again in our lives, we really do not need that negative emotional loop playing again. Gratitude is where it's at, cat! Without it we are endlessly wondering why, and with it we can walk on by!

Grace

It's often said that there is too little love in this world, and whilst this may be true, well I'm not sure that this is the only quality we are lacking. I personally feel that one of the saddest things in this hi-tech world is the lack of grace. That fabulous and beautiful energy of acceptance of who and what we and others are, the unknowing but trusting love of the universe and all of creation, the simple ability to treat others as we would like to be treated, it is a willing acceptance of all that is not limited by our personal desires and problems, that is grace.

We ourselves should seek grace in our lives and then we can access its powerful healing as it removes the need to react to the madding crowd, and takes us far away from its influence, even though we are still here. The essence of grace is not reacting to the troubles and niggling stupidities of the circle world, and of those who are firmly and tightly wrapped in its energy draining tendrils. The world needs more people that think, feel and act and move with grace, purposeful yet bending; like the enduring willow we can drift with the wind, bending but not breaking, no conflict yet true to our purpose. Then others can see that the circle world has them by the short and curlies, as they look on bemused as a graceful person lets people past, opens doors, gives way in traffic, stands in supermarket queues happily.

It behoves us well to aim for grace, to capture it and to hold it close, like a precious but fragile flower that births in us the ability to grow more of the same and to share it with others. We need to learn to carry ourselves through the world with grace, not pride, seeking only to see the beauty of the universe's creation, of the magnificence of the human soul. We can then let go of the reactive mind, and its emotional spats, and its conflicts, and its egocentric self. Instead we can gracefully allow acceptance of all good things, and then there is no resistance to the receiving of positive and loving energy.

I'm not saying that we should strut down the avenue like a supermodel in diaphanous robes that flutter in the breeze, no, not unless we want to of course, what I mean is that we should stop reacting to the bad manners and plain rudeness of others. We should remember that most people are doing their best to break away from the circle world; it's just that nobody has told them about it yet, let alone shown them the way out of it. Whether they know about it or not, we need to diffuse the energy projections that are coming from their uncaring acts, and we don't want to be taking any of their negative energies home with us to affect our lives and H.E.F.'s do we? Grace allows us to ignore their energy whilst still remaining compassionate towards the dilemma that they are in, without grace we meet bad manners with anger and screwed up frowning faces, which is never a good thing.

Grace is always remaining in contact with source energy; it is feeling good even though a cloud has just burst over our heads. It is not complaining at the number of people that dive through when we hold the door open at the shops, it is smiling at the long supermarket queue, it is accepting that war is not our fault and still feeling peace in our hearts. It is wretches like us, having once been lost, being found, and then saved, it is amazing. There's no rush, everything will get done in its sweet time, or it won't, so don't worry, be happy, be graceful, be a being in grace, just be, right now.

Peace

Peace is a state of being, an inner stillness, and an energy statement of non-conflict. It has no opinion other than being here in gratitude and grace but not joining in with the turmoil of the circle world of the ego. It is taking the viewpoint that all of the conflicts in the world that are the core of the circle world, really are not worth the cost and effort of joining in.

Finding peace in our lives will involve some time and effort to extricate ourselves from the world's labyrinth of doing and thinking, and we need to keep up those efforts until we are free. We can all do it, but we just have to make that choice to move away from the action-reaction world of the ego, and into the non-conflict arena of peace.

When we are free from it and in peace, we will be able to help others from the labyrinth of the circle world by being the light that guides them, the beacon that gives them a non-reactive and connected soul to talk to. We are still human, we are still alive and fully physical, we can still do all of the things that we love to do, but our energy has been raised to a higher frequency, and we have crossed the mental plateaux of doubt and insecurity.

Peace is a state of mental and emotional calmness that blocks out the maelstrom of thoughts, ideas and opinions of the circle world. When we first get to this state of peace we have to be a little wary, because it is all too easy to jerk ourselves back to where we started. This can happen because we entertain a negative thought or supposition and follow it back into negative energy; this will pull us back into the circle world with a resounding thump, and suddenly we're not in Kansas anymore.

When we first venture into the higher frequencies we are at a fragile stage, and negative emotional energy can drag us back all too easily, we may see-saw now and then whilst we are letting go of all our negative patterns and heading for a peaceful emotional and mental state. One of the most important things to remember is not to be against anything, and not to oppose things, others' ideas or other people. Here lies conflict and the stuff of the circle world. It is imperative not to be drawn into arguments or to respond to vexatious people, ignore injustice if you can't change it, don't take sides, walk away from negativity; you don't need any of it.

I know that we cannot just ignore other people during this beginning phase, but it is important that we do take the time to be in our own energy, to allow the changes that we have made to settle in our H.E.F.'s. That way we can get used to the way that we feel and perceive energy and the world and others. Opinions and conflict only cloud our perceptions and drag us into mental thought processes that remove us from our healing connection and source energy, throwing us into frustration and the competitive need to solve the problems of people and the world.

Remember that all conflict comes from ego and distance from source energy, and apparent and perceived distance from others and their 'opposing' beliefs. Conflict and anger are of the circle world, they do not, and by their destructive nature cannot produce peace. If something good comes from a conflict it is because someone has decided to do something good after the event. But they could easily have decided to do that good thing without the conflict having to happen; only the circle world could convince us that peace only comes through, and after, conflict.

Contrary to popular opinion, in energy terms, anger does not 'clear the air'; it is simply the voice of a negative energy loop that has built up to explosion point. The 'calm' after the anger and negative expression of the argument is not peace, it is merely the lowest point of the energy loops cycle. You can be assured that as soon as the arguing is over, that the negative emotional energy cycle will reinstate itself and the process will start again. How and when it next happens depends on external circumstances, but unless this energy is cleared, then happen again it will.

Peace is that energy that doesn't require anger or conflict to exist or be, it is simply and beautifully the lack of conflict. Of course the ego will try and convince us that the lack of conflict will make life boring, well far from it; peace allows us to watch the zigzag path of conflict from a distance, happily allowing those that desire to be a part of the circle world to get on with it. Peace justifies nothing but signifies connection and that connection brings great benefits, the first being lack of stress, and the rest being great bonuses.

John Lennon said it best;

"All we are saying is give peace a chance!"

Energy work.

There is no hocus-pocus with energy work it is all about how we live our lives and the choices that we make, and how we deal with the outcomes of those choices. Whether or not we know about, or find out about our H.E.F.'s is actually another choice that we make. We don't have to but it does help to put the way things happen the way that they do into perspective. That subtle energy is all around us and is what we work with to manifest our lives, is by the by in a way. As with all energy work we only have to find out as much as we need to make progress with.

Energy work does not require that we set aside a decade of our lives to contemplate our navels, no, in fact we need only learn that taking responsibility for our past choices and their manifestations here and now, and making better choices works well too. Of course this may take longer to realise full healing and effectiveness, how much longer I don't know, we are all different, as are our emotional blocks. But it is heartening for all to know that energy work is available to everyone, and all the time 24/7. We do not need to be part of a church, a special club, have a license, or buy a special suit, or a medicine- ball or anything.

In fact we need only take responsibility for our lives and free ourselves from the circle world of the ego, easy. Some of us may feel intuitively that we need to take time to gently release blocks and take our own time. This is fine, we should do so, and it's our life and our time to take.

The whole point of energy work is that we become effective and wholly- healed human beings capable of making powerful decisions as an individual, that we take control of our own thoughts, feelings and emotions. We are moving away from being triggered into all too familiar patterns of behaviour that are negative emotional memories from our past. Dr Wayne Dyer has a great expression for this phenomena; he says, "The wake doesn't drive the boat!" What he is saying is that the past should not be driving your life from the back seat.

Achieving our energy freedom may take time, maybe longer than we first thought, but it is time well spent that will repay us over and over again for the rest of our lives. It **is** do-able by all of us, it will take effort, of course it will, but it isn't that hard, especially if we choose to work assiduously with positive intent. It may be our conscious choice that we want to do what we can to make this happen as soon as we can, and this is under-standable given the rewards, but a word of caution to temper our ardour here. Some blocks need time and contemplation to be released; they could entail a series of releases that might involve recuperation each time. We should remember that these blocks took years of unwitting but active negative manifesting to be created and sustained in our energy fields. By attempting a rush job we could cause more problems on top of the original blocks by our expectations exceeding our capacity to move on.

It's a bit like a young man deciding that he is going to be a champion body builder; he reads all the magazines, watches videos of the competitions, he buys the equipment and the gear and sits there wondering where the muscles are! It's going to take longer than that, kid; you've got the equipment, now comes the work. I have given us the basic equipment, and now we have to decide what level of inner work we are going to do. Stating our intents as thoughts is fine, but if our feelings don't match those thoughts then they remain ineffective and are mental lip-service only. To paraphrase a well-known saying, 'the road to healing is paved with good intentions.' Affirmations are great and are very useful to us, but only after we have examined the inner dark feelings and emotional energy blocks that we are intending to change.

Part of our purpose in this world is to decide the way that we are going to work with our inner selves, and how we are going to approach it. Energy work is not just about healing past energy patterns, releasing pain and therefore fixing our H.E.F.'s and connecting to source and healing Earth energy, no, it's also about self-individuation through removing our reliance on the external physical world. Yes, we are in the circle world, and yes, that's what makes the world go round, but it is only when we reach a state of inner calm and stillness that we can know who we are in this world, what we want to contribute to it, and why. Simply becoming a self-realised, own- decision- making individual who is free from the group influences of the circle world is a great gift to the planet, its people, and the universe of subtle energy.

We all owe it to ourselves, our families, our friends, lovers, colleagues, and the world at large to become as free as we can get from the old emotional pain and limited beliefs that the circle world offers. That way we can all serve the world from our best and highest energy place all of the time that we are down here, freeing ourselves from the annoying randomness of the circle world whilst we manifest our lives as we desire them. There is no reason to fear an uncertain world, or an uncertain future, if we ourselves have taken full responsibility for creating our lives consciously. Like the 'ill-fated' *Titanic* we have been steaming in the wrong direction toward icebergs of our own unwitting creation, but life doesn't have to be a disaster, we can change how we feel and think, and thus we can change our lives through the influence of subtle energy. We don't even have to tell anybody else what we are doing, because the whole thing is self-initiated, and is about our relationship with source energy. As I have said many times, we can all tap into source at any time, but it can never be used for evil purpose, nor changed to negative intent.

Subtle energy is a magnificent and beautiful gift from source that is with us and around us at all times, even in the darkest periods of human history source has been there to be turned to. Energy is free of charge, we just have to move positively toward it; then we accept it, allow it, and receive it, then we can bask in the joyful glow of our own creations. Life is always good, the sun is always shining above the clouds, and spring always comes. It is only the circle world that can separate us from the marvellous creation that the immortal soul interred in a human body can be. Negative thoughts, energy, and emotions cannot understand the simplicity of the message of source energy, because their very nature is to create confusion and add complexity through conflict, thus guaranteeing its continued existence in our lives. Ego tells us to forge forwards with action when the healing power of source energy is two steps sideways in calmness and love.

Success as an immortal soul doing time as a human being.

Well here we are, right here in our here and now, we want to start somewhere and that is here. But this book has given us a lot of information that is difficult to take in all at once. OK then, here is a list of some important methods of energy work for us to re-cap. They are in no particular order of importance, but I would read one every day until we are confident that the theory is embedded in our noggins. A good method might be to concentrate on one until we 'know' it, but as always, we should intuit what feels the best for us on that particular day.

Evenness.
Calm the mind, move away from inner emotional reactions of any kind. Stop the emotional roller-coaster and stop applying labels to events. Let everything just be what it is, whether we like it or not. Back away from the circle world reactions of the ego.

Affirmation: *I relinquish control of my life, I trust myself to just be, that is enough.*

"Don't panic!"
When any person or situation seems to be getting beyond our control do not extend outwards with thought, do not frantically search for what to 'do' next. Instead move inside and concentrate our feelings in the base of our stomach, and breathe deeply and slowly.

Affirmation: *I do not need to cope, I simply am, I am simply me, and I trust in myself, and I trust in the universe, all is well.*

Everything is for a reason.
Whatever our level of understanding of the workings of energy and the universe, we have to start from a point of trust, that a higher intelligence is agreeing to work with us, a soul contract for the better. This can take time to turn the ship around, so trust that everything happens for a good reason, even if we can't see it yet.

Affirmation: *The universe is a friendly place, everything and everyone here is working for my good, and I am supported in love and energy.*

Expect the best – Accept the rest.
With our Gratitude, Grace and Peace attitude, we need to also develop a powerful expectancy; we have to know that the things that we desire are happening, and now. If our 'now' doesn't

appear to reflect our desires, then we have to accept it is going to happen, and that means accepting all that is right now.

Affirmation: *Everything that I desire is on its way to me right now, until then I joyfully accept all that is, all is well in universe.*

Meditation – quiet time alone.

Traditionally meditation is seen as sitting in the lotus position and ohming away like a good 'un. With modern, busy lives this isn't always possible. So I see meditation as an inner time that can be done anywhere, it is possible to shut the madding crowd out. Just make sure that if we use music that it doesn't have words or a distracting hook. Shut your eyes and close your thoughts, and repeat this gently.

Affirmation: *All is open to me, all is energy. I am all that is, I am free.*

How do I feel?

The circle world pushes us into a rush of constant doing that seems to require instant responses and choices to situations that we don't feel right about. Too many of these and we don't know who or what we are, resulting in emotional pain. The answer is to check inside before we answer, before we decide, even if somebody is pushing us. If we don't have this time, then work with this mantra to make the time for the next time.

Affirmation: *My time is my own; I decide how I feel, now and always. My heart is energy, my soul is the universe.*

Stop thinking so much.

Thinking too much is the preserve of the circle world, and it is the major ploy of the ego to stop us feeling what we really desire to do. Thinking promotes worry because it makes us constantly compare everything all the time. Thinking is not always your friend, check your feelings too, they are true.

Affirmation: *I do not have any time to waste thinking, instead I will feel, and then I will know 'who' I am and why.*

Thank your body for everything.

Our bodies are amazing; they are the interface that allows us to sense the physical world through all six of our senses. What's the sixth? Energy is the sixth, and the most subtle, but the most powerful. Our bodies can even sense energy, with practice, they are amazing, thank your body every day of your life.

Affirmation: *Thank you body for everything, I love you as you love me, we work together to enjoy every second of this wonderful life, thank you with all my heart.*

Don't be against anything, find things to be for.

When we decide that we are against something, a war perhaps, we are setting up and opposing energy to that war, and that energy is projected at that war, whether we realise it or not. Better to be for peace, be for a peaceful solution that works. Never be against anything, be for a peaceful solution, or just peace.

Affirmation: *I allow the world to rage around me, I am complete, I am here, and I am for peace in gratitude and grace.*

Decide what we really desire from life.

One of the problems with becoming an energy worker is that the things we previously thought important often fall away from us, and we are left wondering. So search your heart now, find the core of what you desire and write down a list of them. Read them to yourself and feel them in your heart. The true ones will stay and grow, whilst the false ones will cease to be important. This way we will always be aiming for what we really desire.

Affirmation: *All that is truly mine come to me now, all that I truly am is revealed to me now, I am in trust and faith, and I am all that I desire and more.*

Acknowledge the soul of every living thing, even the ones that we don't agree with.

Every person, animal, creature and organism alive on this planet is part of the whole, part of the one soul that is everything. We are seeking to improve our souls and our lives, which is a choice; it doesn't make us better than all the villains and bad guys and gals. They are living their lives as they see fit, we must allow that and let them be. We don't have to agree with them, even like them, but at a soul level we must accept that they also have a right to be here. Besides this would be a pretty boring place without the contrast that they provide.

Affirmation: *I am me and I am free, I acknowledge that all are one, all are the one soul, I choose my life, I am me and I am free.*

Patience isn't waiting.

Having patience is often seen as a sweetener for having to wait for the things that we desire. But the simple fact is that the things that we desire have to be manifested too, and that takes time. Patience doesn't make us wait, nor is it an excuse for not having. Patience stops us from creating worry and negative emotion in the interim that *could* push our desires away from us. Be patient, patience is good.

Affirmation: *Virtue of patience flow through me now, allow me to see that all I desire is with me now, I know that patience is immediate and everlasting, I know me.*

Don't make negative statements.

As we increase the speed and strength of our energy fields the chance for little trip-ups before we are healed increases. The ego loves its negative statements, and loves giving life to negative emotional energy, so be careful what you say, and be careful what you agree with that others say. If you do accidentally speak in the negative, use this affirmation.

Cancel these words, cancel their effect in my life, I am manifesting my truth from my heart, I am that which I am.

My path to writing this book has taken me many years of learning and growing, through both positive and negative events. I have manifested my life as I desire it, so I know that you can too. However I know that I couldn't have got to here without my teacher, Hazel Raven and her incredible energy. Whether your path into energy, your own healed energy, requires that you find a teacher, I don't know, we are all different, but I do know that I consciously looked for that teacher.

Your path requires that you do what you really feel to be authentic and true for you, nobody else's path will work, it may for a while, but sooner rather than later you will be left wishing that you had blazed your own trail. Start with books, there are many that will guide you, I won't presume to tell you what to read, but I reckon that for a start you can't go wrong with any book by these people: Dr Wayne Dyer and Stuart Wilde, Hazel Raven, and whomsoever that you may feel guided to read.

Thank you for accompanying me on this short journey into the world of energy work, I bless you and your soul, and I wish you the happiness that you truly desire. I hope that we meet again in other books, and that your light can shine ever so brightly into this world, you are needed and welcomed.

Shine on you, crazy diamonds.

Thank you.

Steve Oakes. Northern England. November 2008.

BOOKS

O is a symbol of the world, of oneness and unity. In different cultures it also means the "eye," symbolizing knowledge and insight. We aim to publish books that are accessible, constructive and that challenge accepted opinion, both that of academia and the "moral majority."

Our books are available in all good English language bookstores worldwide. If you don't see the book on the shelves ask the bookstore to order it for you, quoting the ISBN number and title. Alternatively you can order online (all major online retail sites carry our titles) or contact the distributor in the relevant country, listed on the copyright page.

See our website **www.o-books.net** for a full list of over 500 titles, growing by 100 a year.

And tune in to myspiritradio.com for our book review radio show, hosted by June-Elleni Laine, where you can listen to the authors discussing their books.

mySpiritRadio